Speaking Better French

The
Key Words and Expressions
You'll Need Every Day

Saul H. Rosenthal

Speaking Better French: The Key Words and Expressions You'll Need Every Day

Published by Wheatmark™
610 East Delano Street, Suite 104, Tucson, Arizona 85705 U.S.A.
www.wheatmark.com

ISBN: 978-1-58736-837-0
LCCN: 2007925282

Also by Saul H. Rosenthal:

The Rules for the Gender of French Nouns

Speaking Better French - Faux Amis

Acknowledgements

I wish to thank Sylvie Shurgot and Evelyne Verneret who each kindly devoted the time to read the entire manuscript and to help me find errors. I especially wish to thank Jean-Marc Bard who sat down and went over the entire manuscript page by page with me discussing nuances of meaning. And finally I wish to thank my wife Cindy, who again was patient during all the time I invested in writing this book. I appreciate her constant support.

Contents

Introduction

I've written this book to help you talk more fluent French, the French that French people use.

I've done this in two ways. The first is by selecting the key words, key expressions, and little idioms that are used all the time in day-to-day conversation. These are the words that make the language flow. In this book I discuss each one separately and tell you how to use it. For each key word or expression I also usually give you a number of examples using it in sentences so you can see how it's normally used. That way, it won't be just a meaningless term for you to memorize.

There are thousands of idioms in French, but many of them are used just occasionally and for very specific occasions.

Take, for instance, the English expressions "There are many ways to skin a cat" and "He's sowing his wild oats". They are nice to know, and there are specific circumstances where they are appropriate to use. However, you could get along very well most of your life in English without knowing those idioms.

French has lots of idioms like that too. *Il fait les quatre cent coups* is pretty close to "He's sowing his wild oats". It's nice if you know it, but you can get along very well without it. It's an idiom that you might encounter just once or twice in your lifetime. You might be able to recognize it but you would probably never recall it fast enough to use it yourself.

However there are other key words and expressions in French that are used all the time. They are the French equivalents of expressions like "just in case", "as soon as", "on the other hand", "all the same", and many, many more.

As opposed to idioms like "sowing his wild oats", which are restricted to once or twice in a lifetime situations, these expressions are multipurpose. They serve in an infinite number of daily situations. You not only need to recognize them, **you need to use them yourself** in daily speech.

These key words are the subjects of this book. Some of them are actual short idioms. Most are simply the words that grease the wheels of French conversation. To have them at your disposal is the difference between being able to say just a simple noun-verb-object French phrase like

John saw the red bicycle

or a flowing sentence like

As soon as John saw the red bicycle about which his mother had spoken...

While the first goal of the book is to give you these little words and expressions that make the language flow, the second goal of the book is to help you talk and understand spoken French.

When I say spoken French, I mean the way people really talk. Some expressions that French people use are very informal, they use short cuts, and they are not what you would call standard or proper French. It's similar to the same informal devices we use in English.

When we say "See you tomorrow!" there is no subject in that sentence. The "I will" has been dropped. We know it's not proper English and we wouldn't use it in a formal letter or a formal interview, but that's the way we often talk.

Most French people use the same kind of abbreviations in casual speech. Most of my French friends think of it as spoken French, as opposed to written French, and accept it as normal, depending on the circumstances.

The French in general tend to be much more purist about their language than we are about English. They've had the grammar pounded into their heads when they were in school and they know immediately which form is standard French. However, when they are speaking they use spoken French, which is different. This book will help you to understand and speak spoken French the way the French speak it.

Consider the expression *"C'est pas vrai !"* It's not standard French because the *"ne"* is dropped, as often happens in spoken French. In standard written French it should be: *"Ce n'est pas vrai"*.

However, in practice almost no one says *Ce n'est pas vrai !* The usual spoken expression is: *C'est pas vrai !* When an expression like *"C'est pas vrai"* is in common use, and when this is the overwhelming way that it's used orally, I include it that way in the book.

You must be aware, however, that in formal situations, and when you are writing something formal, you must use standard French.

To help you remember, where I use informal spoken French like this in the book, I usually call it to your attention in the text with a little reminder that this is spoken French and should not be used in more formal situations.

My hope is that you will not only find this book a great resource, but that it will also be fun for you to read. Now go ahead and get started.

Key Words and Expressions

I have not alphabetized the key words on purpose. This is not meant to be dictionary. My hope is that these expressions will interest and surprise you as you encounter them, and that the book will be a book of discovery and a pleasure to read. And, rest assured, there is an alphabetical listing of the expressions in the back of the book for reference, in case you ever need it.

Please note that when there is dialogue, in most cases I have adopted the convention of placing a dash between the two speakers. For example: *Tu peux venir ? --- J'espère bien !*

Let's begin:

Qui sait !

Qui sait ! means "Who knows!" and can be used in the same way that you'd use "Who knows!" in English.

À combien vont ils arriver ? --- Qui sait !

How many will show up? --- Who knows!

Va savoir !

Va savoir could be translated, like *Qui sait*, as "Who knows".

However while *Qui sait !* can be used for any unknown simple fact, *Va savoir !* has more the feeling of an unsolved (and unsolvable) small mystery. It means something more like "We'll never know!".

> *Est-ce qu'elle a vraiment fait ça ? --- Va savoir !*

> Did she really do that? --- We'll never know.

quant à ...

The expression *quant à* means "as for" or "with regard to". *Quant à* often, but not always, begins a sentence. As with most of the expressions which I will give you here, *quant à* is versatile in the sense that it can be used in many different circumstances:

> *Quant à moi, je suis d'accord.*

> As for me, I agree.

> *Quant à ces maisons, je crois qu'elles sont chères.*

> As for these houses, I think that they are expensive.

> *Quant à la morale, elle ne me préoccupe guère. Je vous scandalise ?*

As for morals, I don't worry about them much. Do I shock you? (from Les Thibault by Roger Martin du Gard)

Quant à y aller le nuit, personne n'ose le faire.

As for going there at night, nobody dares to do it.

par hasard

Par hasard means "by accident" or "by chance".

Je l'ai rencontré par hasard.

I met him by chance.

Est-ce que, par hasard, tu pourrais le faire pour moi ?

Can you do it for me, by any chance?

Par le plus grand des hasards j'ai retrouvé ce livre.

By extraordinary luck I found this book again.

By an extraordinary accident I found this book again.

pourvu que

Pourvu que means "Provided that" or "Let's hope that" and it expresses a wish. It usually starts a sentence or clause and is used with the subjunctive of the next verb. It's a figurative use of the verb *pourvoir* (to provide).

> *Pourvu qu'elle arrive à l'heure ! Nous pourrions alors manger à huit heures.*

> Provided that she arrives on time, we'd be able to eat at eight o'clock.

> Let's hope that she arrives on time. If so we can eat at eight o'clock.

> *Pourvu qu'il puisse venir !*

> Let's hope that he can come!

> *Pourvu qu'il fasse beau !*

> Let's hope that the weather is good!

Quel... !

This exclamation is translated as "What a..." and usually expresses admiration as in:

> *Quel repas !*

> What a meal!

> *Quelle femme !*

> What a woman!

This expression can, however, sometimes express a negative sentiment as in:

16

Quel désastre !

What a disaster!

Quelle horreur !!!

This is a very French expression and is usually spoken with lots of emotion and emphasis. It means, naturally: "That's horrible!" or "How horrible!"

> *Elle a vraiment dit ça ? Quelle horreur !!*
>
> She really said that? How horrible!

un sacré...

The *adjective* sacré is ordinarily placed after the noun it modifies, in which case it means "sacred". For example: *un édifice sacré.*

However, in casual spoken French, when you place *sacré* before the noun as an exclamation and call something *"un sacré..."* it means "a heck of a..." or, more vulgarly, "a damn...".

> *C'était un sacré travail.*
>
> It was a heck of a (tough) job.
>
> *Pierre est un sacré casse-pieds !*
>
> Pierre is a damn pain in the neck.
>
> *Sacré Maurice, il nous étonnera toujours !*

Maurice is incredible, he always astonishes us!

Good old Maurice, he keeps astonishing us!

trop

Trop usually means "too much" and thus has a slightly negative connotation.

However, when used to modify a positive adjective or adverb, and spoken with enthusiasm, *trop* doesn't mean "too much". On the contrary, it intensifies the positive adjective or adverb and can be translated more like "wonderfully" or "extraordinarily".

This is a very slangy usage, but it's used all the time in everyday speech, especially by young people.

Ta robe est trop belle !

Il est trop beau !

Ce film était trop bien !

Le poisson est trop bon !

Elle est trop mignonne !

Il est trop sympa !

Trop beau !

Trop bon !

Je veux bien

Je veux bien means "I'd be glad to" but is usually used with a "but" when there is some obstacle to you doing it, as in:

Je veux bien le faire mais je n'ai pas le temps.

I'd be glad to do it but I don't have the time.

Je veux bien les arroser mais je ne trouve pas le tuyau.

I'd be glad to water them but I can't find the hose.

Je veux bien conduire mais je ne connais pas la route.

I'd be glad to drive but I don't know the route.

It's also used in response to a request, again meaning "I'd be glad to".

Est-ce que tu peux le faire pour moi ? --- Oui, je veux bien !

Could you do it for me? --- Yes, I'd be glad to!

D'accord !

This is the French equivalent of "OK" or "I agree". It's

used all the time and you will find occasions to use it many times a day.

"D'accord" is short for *"Je suis d'accord."* You can usually use either one. *Je suis d'accord* is just a little more formal. For example:

> *Je suis d'accord pour aller au Restaurant Provençal ce soir.*
>
>> It's okay with me for the Restaurant Provençal this evening.
>
> *On va au Restaurant Provençal ce soir ? --- D'accord.*
>
>> Shall we go to the Restaurant Provençal this evening? --- Okay.
>
> *Est-ce que tu peux acheter du pain pour moi ? --- D'accord.*
>
>> Can you buy some bread for me? Okay.
>
> *Je ne suis pas d'accord.*
>
>> I don't agree.
>
> *Ils sont d'accord.*
>
>> They agree. They are in agreement.

In very slangy speech you may even hear *d'accord* added to the americanism "okay", as in:

> *Okay, d'accord !*

or even, believe it or not:

Okay, d'ac !

I would recommend that you **don't** use *okay d'accord,* even if you should hear it from others. You are, after all, trying to sound more French, not more American.

C'est pas évident

C'est pas évident means "It's not evident (or obvious) how to do it (or even whether it can be done)" or "It's doubtful. It might not work".

On peut peut-être le faire, mais c'est pas évident.

Maybe it can be done, but it's not obvious / but I doubt it / but I'm not sure.

Est-ce que tu crois qu'on peut nager ici ? --- Avec autant de rochers, c'est pas évident.

Do you think that one can swim here? --- With so many rocks I'm not sure.

Although the *ne* is usually dropped from *C'est pas évident* in spoken French, it would not be considered standard French. If you are in a more formal situation, say: *Ce n'est pas évident.*

c'est-à-dire

You use the expression *c'est-à-dire* to make something that you have already said more precise. You could translate it by "that is", or by "that is to say", (which turns out to be the literal translation).

> *J'arriverai à l'heure prévue. C'est-à-dire, à huit heure pile.*
>
> > I'll arrive at the agreed upon time. That is to say right at eight o'clock.

> *Pour me baigner dans la piscine, je préfère que l'eau soit plutôt chaude. C'est-à-dire, plus de vingt-six degrés.*
>
> > To swim in the pool I prefer the water to be rather warm. That is to say, more than twenty-six degrees.

> *Le lendemain, c'est-à-dire mardi, nous...*
>
> > The next day, that is, Tuesday, we...

C'est-à-dire ? (with a question mark) means "Could you clarify?" or "Could you be more precise?". For example:

> *- La réponse est arrivé trois semaines après l'envoi de ma lettre.*

> *- C'est-à-dire ?*

> *- Début décembre.*

Note that in more formal language one would say <u>Au</u>

début de décembre, but in spoken French you'd be more likely to hear *Début décembre*.

à savoir

À savoir means "namely", or "that is to say", and thus is a synonym for *c'est-à-dire*.

> **Il lui manque quelque chose d'essentiel, à savoir l'intelligence.**
>
> > He lacks something essential, namely intelligence.
> >
> > He lacks something essential, that's to say: intelligence.
> >
> > He lacks something essential, if you want to know: intelligence.
>
> **Ils ont beaucoup d'avantages. --- À savoir?**
>
> > They have alot of advantages. --- That's to say? / Namely? / Could you clarify?

j'ai ouï dire (que)

While some of our expressions come from casual French, using *j'ai ouï dire* may give people the impression that you speak an unusually refined and elegant French. It comes from an old classic French verb, *ouïr* (to hear), which is now mostly obsolete except for this expression. The sense of hearing, however, is still called *l'ouïe*.

J'ai ouï dire means "I've heard it said", and may refer to a rumor or to a word-of-mouth piece of information. It's often used in a light-hearted, joking manner.

> *J'ai ouï dire que sa soeur est très belle.*
>
> > I've heard it said that his sister is very beautiful.
>
> *J'ai ouï dire que tu es très malin.*
>
> > I've heard that you're very shrewd.
>
> *J'ai ouï dire que tu vas vendre ta maison.*
>
> > I've heard that you are going to sell your house.
>
> A French synonym for *j'ai ouï dire* would be *j'ai entendu dire.*

Il s'agit (de)

> The verb *agir* by itself means to act or to take an action, but *il s'agit (de)* is translated "It's a question of" or "it's about" or "it's a matter of". It's a very common expression and you will hear it all the time.
>
> > *De quoi s'agit-il ?* or *Il s'agit de quoi ?*
> >
> > > What's it about? What's it a question of? What's the matter?
> >
> > *Il s'agit de ma santé.*
> >
> > > It deals with my health.

Il s'agit de Jacques.

It's about Jacques.

Il ne s'agit pas d'argent.

It's not a question of money.

Quand il s'agit de boire un coup, il est toujours le premier.

When it's a question of having a drink, he's always the first.

à peu près

The French expression *à peu près* means just about, approximately, more-or-less, nearly, pretty close to. It's used in expressions like:

Il est à peu près certain que...

It's almost certain that...

Le restaurant était à peu près vide.

The restaurant was practically empty.

Il y avait à peu près cinquante personnes dans le magasin.

There were close to fifty people in the store.

faire les courses
faire du shopping

Faire les courses means to run errands or go shopping for food and supplies. You will use it, or hear it, just about every day.

> *Nous allons faire les courses demain matin.*
>
> > We are going to run our errands tomorrow morning.

If you are talking about wandering about shopping malls and shopping for clothes, that is *faire du shopping*.

> *Ma femme aime beaucoup faire du shopping, moi pas du tout.*
>
> > My wife likes very much to go shopping but I don't like it at all.

Faire du shopping is of course imported from English and a French language purist might be aghast to find it in a book, but I'm giving you what people really say. And, they do say *faire du shopping*.

C'est pas vrai !

The expression *C'est pas vrai !* is said with incredulity and astonishment, and with an accent on the *"C'est"* and one especially on the *"vrai"*. Either the *"C'est"* or the *"vrai!"*, or both, may be slightly drawn out, depending on the dramatic flair of the speaker.

C'est pas vrai ! means something like "It can't be true!" or "You've got to be kidding!" It's wonderfully expressive.

> *Elle a dit ça ? C'est pas vrai !*

> She said that? You've <u>got</u> to be kidding!

Jamais de la vie !

This expression literally says something like "Never in my life" and colloquially means something like "No way!" or "Not a chance!"

> *Votre mère veut venir vivre chez nous? Jamais de la vie !*

> Your mother wants to come live with us? No way!

Impeccable !

In French, *impeccable !* is used as a freestanding exclamation and means "Perfect!". It can also be used in a sentence with the same meaning.

Where in English impeccable is pronounced with an accent on the "pecc" and the "able" is somewhat swallowed, in French the *"ab"*, at least, of the *"able"*, is fully pronounced.

In casual speech, *"Impeccable"* is sometimes shortened to *"Impec !"*, especially by young people.

> *Comment était le diner ? --- Impeccable !*

How was the dinner? --- Perfect! / Great!

Je peux arriver à vingt heures. --- Impec !

I can arrive at eight o'clock. --- Perfect!

C'était impeccable, ton idée.

Your idea was sensational.

Impeccable can also mean perfectly dressed or perfectly clean, as in English.

> *un complet impeccable*

>> a suit of clothes perfect for the occasion (and attractive, clean and uncrushed)

tant pis

The expression *tant pis* means "Too bad!" or "So much the worse!", (which is it's literal translation). It is often used in a light vein, slightly humorously.

> *Nous ne pouvons pas aller avec vous au restaurant ce soir. --- Tant pis pour vous, c'est un très bon resto.*

> We can't go with you to the restaurant this evening. --- Too bad for you. It's a very good restaurant.

> *Il ne veut pas se balader avec nous. --- Tant pis pour lui !*

28

He doesn't want to go walking with us. ---
Too bad for him. (It's he that's missing out.)

Sometimes *tant pis* can just mean "Never mind, don't worry, it's not a big deal". (You can tell from context and tone of voice.)

Désolé, je peux pas jouer au tennis avec vous demain. --- Oh, dommage ! Tant pis.

Sorry, I can't play tennis with you tomorrow. --- Oh! Too bad, never mind, don't worry.

Note that the *ne* was left out of the *je peux pas* in the last example. I know that I've explained it before but this is casual French. In more formal situations you'd have to say: *Je suis désolé, mais je ne peux pas jouer...*

tant mieux

Tant mieux is the opposite of *tant pis. Tant mieux* means "So much the better!"

Jean peut venir avec nous demain. --- Tant mieux, j'aime marcher avec lui.

Jean can come with us tomorrow. --- So much the better. I enjoy walking with him.

voire

The adverb *voire* is used when you have made an assertion and you want to make it stronger. *Voire* can be translated as "even", "indeed", or "nay!". It's a very useful expression. Here are some examples:

> *Elle est agaçante, voire horrible, de temps en temps.*
>
>> She's annoying, nay, horrible, from time to time.
>
> *Durant des mois, voire des années...*
>
>> For months, even years...
>
> *Dire cela est inutile, voire dangereux.*
>
>> To say that is useless, indeed dangerous.

Voire has nothing to do with the verb *voir* (to see).

Elle est comment ? or *Comment est-elle ?*

This can mean "What's she like?", "What kind of person is she?", or "What does she look like?". It's used only for people, not for places or things.

> *Elle est comment, ta copine ?*
>
>> What is your girlfriend like? And what does she look like?
>
> *Votre frère, comment est-il ?*
>
>> What's your brother like? What kind of person is he? How's your brother's health? (if the speaker knew that your brother had been sick).

bien (used to intensify)

The adverb *bien* is often used to intensify another adverb or an adjective. It can be translated as "quite", "very", or "really". A French synonym would be *vraiment*.

Here are some examples of the use of *bien* to modify an adverb or an adjective.

> *Elle est bien jeune.*
>
> > She's quite young.
>
> *C'est bien assez.*
>
> > It's quite enough. It's really enough.
>
> *C'est bien mieux.*
>
> > It's really better. It's much better.

Here are some examples of the use of *bien* to modify various verbs.

> *Tu peux venir ? --- J'espère bien !*
>
> > Can you come? --- I really hope so.
>
> *J'espère bien y aller.*
>
> > I really hope to go.
>
> *Je veux bien le faire.*
>
> > I'm quite willing to do it. I really want to do it.

Il faut bien le faire.

It's really necessary to do it.

Il me semble bien que...

It really seems to me that...

Paul est bien venu, n'est-ce pas ?

Paul really came, didn't he? Paul *did* come, didn't he?

Note that in other contexts, bien means "well".

Nous allons bien manger.

We will eat well.

J'ai bien dormi.

I have slept well.

correct

You can use the French adjective *correct* to mean "accurate" or "correct" as in English.

Toutes ses réponses ont été correctes.

All her answers were correct.

However, *correct* can also often mean "proper", "polite" or "honest in dealings".

Il a été correct avec Jean.

He was polite and fair with Jean.

M. Blanc est toujours correct en affaires.

Mr. Blanc is always honest in business dealings.

However, in spoken French, *correct* has another meaning. If you are talking, for example, about a restaurant, a hotel, a meal or a wine, *c'était correct* means that it was acceptable and reasonable, and that there was nothing wrong with it, but that it was not special. For example:

Comment était le restaurant hier soir? --- euh... C'était correct.

This lets you know that the restaurant was passable and okay, but not special.

exceptionnellement

In English, exceptionally means "unusually" (as in exceptionally hot) or "exceedingly" (as in exceptionally intelligent). *Exceptionnellement* can have these same meanings in French.

However, the way you are most likely to encounter *exceptionnellement* is different than what you would expect from English. In French, *exceptionnellement* often means "for this time only", "by way of an exception". For example:

Le magasin est exceptionnellement fermé ce mardi pour raisons familiales.

The store is closed this Tuesday only, for family reasons.

donc

Donc is an expressive word much used in spoken French. Although its meaning is almost always evident when I hear it, it's difficult to define exactly. I'll do my best, and then give you some examples which I hope will clarify the usage.

The first meaning of *donc* is "thus" or "therefore". After an initial thought *donc* introduces the conclusion which is a consequence of the initial thought.

Je pense, donc je suis.

I think, therefore I am. (Déscartes)

Il a téléphoné pour dire qu'il est très en retard, donc nous allons manger sans lui.

He telephoned to say that he will be very delayed, therefore we will eat without him.

Il a trois grandes maisons, il est donc assez riche.

He has three big houses. He is thus fairly rich.

The second usage of *donc* is to give emphasis or to reinforce a question or an exclamation. It may express surprise in this usage. It can be translated as "thus" but it can often be almost omitted in the translation.

C'est donc ici que tu travailles ?

> It's (thus) here that you work? So this is where you work? (with surprise)

Qu'est-ce que vous voulez, donc ?

> What exactly do you want? (Said with emphasis in an upset tone of voice.)

Donc, il n'est pas venu ?

> (Thus), he didn't come !? (with incredulity).

Taisez-vous, donc!

> Shut up, will you !?

Dans sa déposition, donc, elle prétend qu'elle n'était pas là.

> In her deposition, thus, she claims that she wasn't there.

C'est cela que je ne comprends pas. --- Mais quoi donc ?

> That's what I don't understand. --- But <u>what</u> exactly?

Finally, *donc* is used after an interruption to come back to the subject.

Vous disiez donc que...

> Thus, you were saying that...

par contre
en revanche
au contraire

Par contre means "on the other hand" and you can use it just as you would use "on the other hand" in English.

> *Il n'est pas très intelligent. Par contre, il est rusé.*

>> He's not very intelligent. On the other hand, he's cunning.

En revanche is a near synonym for *par contre*, and also means "on the other hand".

> *La mobylette a un pneu crevé, mais en revanche le vélo est en état de marche. Si tu veux tu peux la prendre.*

>> The moped has a flat tire but on the other hand the bicycle is ready to go. If you want to, you can take it.

The expression *au contraire* is slightly different, as it means "on the contrary" and expresses more opposition.

> *Jacques n'est pas intelligent. --- Au contraire! Je le trouve très intelligent.*

>> Jacques isn't intelligent. --- On the contrary, I find him very intelligent.

en contrepartie

The expression *en contrepartie* means "in compensation for" or "in return". For example:

> *La pluie avait cessé. En contrepartie, le vent avait commencé à souffler fort.*

>> The rain had stopped. On the other hand the wind had started to blow strongly.

Note that *en contrepartie* is not quite the same as *par contre* or *en revanche*, which mean on the other hand. *En contrepartie* means "in compensation for", implying that while something was taken away, something else was added to balance it or compensate for it:

> *Elle n'était pas jolie, mais en contrepartie elle était intelligente et sympathique.*

>> She wasn't pretty, but in compensation, she was intelligent and likeable.

En contrepartie is a bit more sophisticated expression than *par contre* and you'll hear it less often in common speech.

Mettons que...
Disons que...

These two expressions mean "Let's say that...". They are used just as you would use "Let's say that" in English. In other words they express the thought "Let's start with this supposition or hypotheses and let's see what comes next."

> *Mettons que je vienne le semaine prochaine. Qu'est-ce que nous allons faire ?*

>> Let's say that can I could come next week. What is it that we are going to do?

> *Disons qu'il l'a fait. Il faut savoir pourquoi.*

>> Let's say that he did it. We need to know why.

Note that *mettons que* uses the subjunctive of the next verb, *(je vienne* in the example above).

As an aside, *mettons que* comes from the verb *admettre*, to admit or acknowledge, but the *ad-* is usually erased from *admettons que* in daily language.

faire (meaning to look, seem, or act like)

Faire is commonly used in this idiomatic sense, meaning: to appear, seem, act like, look like. For example:

> *Ne fais pas l'idiot !*

>> Don't act like an idiot!

> *Il ne fait pas soixante ans.*

>> He doesn't appear sixty years old. He doesn't seem sixty.

> *Elle fait plus jeune que son âge.*

She seems younger than her age.

dont

Like *donc, dont* is one of the little words that lubricates the language and makes it flow. It means "of which" or "about which". (It can also be translated "of whom" or "in which", but if you remember "of which" the other meanings will be self evident).

Les sujets dont je veux parler sont...

> The subjects about which I wish to speak are...

Il y a deux arbres dont l'un est un cerisier.

> There are two trees, of which one is a cherry tree.

Il y avait six invités, dont Jacques faisait partie.

> There were six guests, of which Jacques was one.

Et voici Marie, ma fille dont je suis si fier.

> And here is Marie, my daughter of whom I am so proud.

Je n'aime pas la façon dont il me parle.

> I don't like the way in which he talks to me.

au cas où...
à tout hasard

The expression *au cas où* means "just in case". It is used frequently in spoken French, and in pretty much the same ways that we would use "just in case".

> *Je vais prendre une veste, au cas où.*

> I'll take a jacket, just in case.

> *Il faut être là, au cas où il arriverait ce soir.*

> We should be there, in case he arrives this evening.

À tout hasard is a synonym.

> *Je vais prendre une veste, à tout hasard.*

> I'll take a jacket, just in case.

c'est pas la peine

This is another very common expression in spoken French. It means "it's not worth the trouble" or "Don't bother".

> *Je vais aller chercher encore du pain. --- C'est pas la peine.*

> I'll go get some more bread. --- It's not worth the trouble. (We have enough of it).

C'est pas la peine d'aller au magasin. Nous en avons assez.

It's not worth the trouble of going to the store. We have enough of it.

C'est pas la peine de lui demander. C'est sûr, il va refuser.

It's not worth the trouble to ask him. It's certain that he will refuse.

Again, this is spoken French. if you are in a more formal situation, you have to say: *Ce n'est pas la peine* (reinserting the *n'*). In practice, what you'll hear is: *C'est pas la peine.*

haut de gamme
bas de gamme

La gamme is the range, of products, colors, articles, etc. *C'est un produit haut de gamme* means it's top of the line, top quality, top of the range. *Bas de gamme* naturally means the opposite.

C'est un ordinateur haut de gamme.

That computer is top quality.

Cette voiture est chère, mais c'est une voiture haut de gamme.

That car is expensive but it's a car which is top of the line.

C'est bon marché, mais c'est du bas de gamme.

It's cheap but it's poor quality.

C'est une émission bas de gamme.

It's an awful TV program.

à mon avis

This expression is in constant use as it means "In my opinion...", and French people have opinions about nearly everything.

À mon avis, c'est stupide.

In my opinion, it's stupid.

Il n'arrivera pas à l'heure, à mon avis.

He won't come on time, in my opinion.

Qu'est-ce qu'on doit faire, à ton avis ?

What should we do, in your opinion?

Il change d'avis comme de chemise.

He changes his opinions like his shirts.

à vrai dire

The expression *à vrai dire* means "to tell you the truth", or "speaking frankly". It usually precedes or follows some unpleasant truth.

Je m'en doutais, à vrai dire.

I suspected it, to tell the truth.

À vrai dire, je crains qu'il ne rate l'épreuve.

Frankly speaking, I fear that he is going to fail the test..

Since *rater* is a bit informal, in a more formal situation you'd say:

À vrai dire, je crains qu'il n'échoue à l'épreuve.

Although, as I said, *à vrai dire* is usually used with a negative thought, it can occasionally be used with a compliment.

À vrai dire, je la trouve assez belle.

To tell the truth, I find her pretty attractive.

Entendu !
Bien entendu !

Entendu literally means "Understood!" and is used somewhat like *D'accord,* but there are nuances of difference.

First of all, *Entendu* can mean that something has been explained to you and you have grasped it:

Ce serait bien que tu sois là pour midi, mais avant il faut que tu ailles à la boulangerie pour le pain et le dessert. --- Entendu !

It would be good if you could get here by noon, but before that you have to go by the bakery for the bread and the dessert. --- Understood!

Secondly, *Entendu* can mean that something has been discussed and decided and you are in agreement. After the discussion you can say:

Entendu !

Agreed! Decided!

C'est entendu !

It's agreed !

or more formally:

C'est une affaire entendue !

It's a deal. It's an agreed deal.

You can see how this differs from *D'accord*, which can be used in reply to a simple question like "Can you come for dinner tomorrow?" and means "Okay".

Finally, *bien entendu* means "sure" or "of course". It can be used alone as an exclamation, or in a sentence.

Vous serez là ? --- Bien entendu !

You'll be there? --- Of course!

Je suis arrivé à cinq heures mais, bien entendu, elle était partie à cinq heures moins le quart.

I had arrived at five o'clock, but of course, she had left at a quarter to five.

Et, bien entendu, je te paierai un bon prix.

And, of course, I will pay you a good price.

And let it be understood, I will pay you a good price.

quand même

The expression *quand même* means "nevertheless", "all the same", or "even so". You can use it pretty much whenever you would use one of these expressions in English.

Quand même, il aurait pu nous prévenir.

All the same, he could have let us know in advance.

Il m'a déconseillé de m'éloigner. --- Vous êtes parti quand même ?

He warned me not to leave. --- You left even so?

Quand même, ça serait gentil de l'acheter pour elle en cadeau.

Even so, it would be nice to buy it for her as a gift.

Il ne fait pas très froid maintenant, mais quand même, je vais apporter une veste.

It's not very cold right now, but even so, I'm going to bring a jacket.

Tu as raison, ça monte très peu. Mais, ça monte quand même.

You are right, it (the slope) rises very little. But it rises nonetheless. (Heard bicycling).

When said as an exclamation, with a tone of humorous protest, it can be translated as "All the same!" or "Really!"

Je sais que tu as faim Jean Marc, mais quand même !

I know you're hungry Jean Marc, but really! (aren't you overdoing it?).

Il fait froid, mais quand même, avec trois pulls tu exagères un peu !

It's cold, but all the same, wearing three sweaters is a bit excessive!

tout de même

Tout de même is a synonym for *quand même*. It means "all the same" and can be used pretty much the same way as *quand même*. *Quand même* is more common but both are used.

Tout de même, il aurait pu nous prévenir.

All the same, he could have let us know in advance.

exagérer

The verb *exagérer* can mean "to exaggerate" but it also often has an idiomatic meaning.

Tu exagères (you are exaggerating) is used in everyday speech to say "That's a bit much!" or "That's a bit excessive" or "You've got to be kidding". It implies that the person addressed is doing something excessive and it suggests a bit of incredulity coupled with mild disapproval.

> *Je vais en acheter trois. --- Tu exagère un peu / Il ne faut pas exagérer*

>> I'm going to buy three of them. --- You are going a bit overboard / Don't overdo it.

> *C'est son troisième dessert. --- Il exagère un peu.*

>> It's his third dessert. --- He's being a bit excessive.

Tu exagères meaning "That's a bit excessive" differs from "You are exaggerating" in ordinary English usage in two ways.

First, in English, "You are exaggerating" means exclusively that you are **describing something unrealistically** (as better, worse, bigger, smaller, etc than it really is). On the other hand, *Tu exagères* means that you are **being excessive** (in what you are saying or doing).

Second, *Tu exagères* in French can refer to excessive action and behavior as well as to speech, while in English "you are exaggerating" is pretty much restricted to speech.

comme (meaning "as a")

Comme generally means "like" or "as", and can be used in a number of senses. In the sense we will discuss here, it means "as a" in the sense of "in the role of". The following examples should make it clear.

> *Elle travaille comme secrétaire.*

>> She is working **as a** secretary / in the role of secretary. (Note that since *comme* here means "as <u>a</u>", the indirect object *une* is not needed and is omitted before *secrétaire*).

> *Il était contremaître. Depuis qu'il a démissionné il travaille comme ouvrier.*

>> He was a foreman but since he quit he has been working **as a** common laborer.

> *Comme plombier il est nul, mais comme électricien il est excellent.*

>> **As a** plumber he's terrible but he's an excellent electrician.

> *Comme gérant, il est efficace.*

As a manager, he does a good job.

Above we are using *comme* in the sense "as a" meaning "in the role of".

On the other hand, we can use *comme* to simply mean "as". In this case, we do follow it with the article *un* or *une*, as you'll see below.

> *Cette maison est grande comme un château.*

> That house is as big **as** a chateau.

> *Est-ce que je dois l'emballer comme un cadeau.*

> Should I wrap it **as** a present.

tout comme

Comme normally means like or as, and *tout comme* adds emphasis and means "<u>just</u> like" or "almost the same as". *Tout comme* is a common expression in spoken French. Synonyms would be *presque* and *presque pareil*.

> *Est-ce que le repas est prêt ? --- C'est tout comme.*

> Is the meal ready? --- It's just about.

> *Ton comportement est tout comme celui d'un bébé.*

> Your behavior is just like that of a baby. (Mother talking to a child).

> You are behaving like a baby.

Sa robe est tout comme la tienne.

Her dress is just like yours.

Her dress is exactly the same as yours.

comme il faut

This is another very common expression using *comme*. It can refer to a place or person and acts as an adjective phrase meaning "as it should be" or "proper".

It can also modify a verb and act as an adverb phrase meaning "as it should be" or "properly".

Tout était comme il faut.

Everything was just as it should be.

C'est un restaurant comme il faut.

It's a restaurant that is just as it should be. (This is meant as a compliment).

Vous êtes habillé comme il faut.

You are dressed just right / just as you should be / very properly.

Ça se fait

This expression is very useful. It says that something "is done", meaning that it's acceptable or proper to do it. The expression is usually used in the negative, as in :

Cela ne se fait pas.

That's not done. That's not acceptable behavior.

Or very casually, as:

Ça se fait pas !

That's not done!

Mâcher du chewing-gum ne se fait pas ici.

It's not proper to chew gum here.

Est-ce qu'on peut manger les côtes d'agneau avec les doigts ? --- Oui. Ça se fait.

Can one eat lamb chops with ones fingers? --- Yes. That's done / acceptable.

En Angleterre, les gens envoient souvent avec la carte de Nöel une longue lettre pour raconter les évènements de l'année écoulée. Oui, ça se fait.

In England, people often send a long letter with their Christmas card to recount all the events of the past year. Yes that's done (acceptable).

ça se dit

The counterpart of *ça se fait* is *ça se dit*.

Est-ce qu'on peut dire ... en français ? --- Oui, ça se dit comme ça.

Can one say ... in French? --- Yes. That's said like that.

However, like *ça se fait, ça se dit* is used more often in the negative, as:

Cela ne se dit pas en bon français !

That's not said in good French!

More casually, it's *ça se dit pas,* as in :

Ça se dit pas ! C'est vulgaire.

One doesn't say that! It's vulgar.

à la rigueur
à la limite

À la rigueur and *à la limite* both mean: if worse comes to worst, in a pinch, if I have to, if I must, if it comes to that, if necessary.

À la rigueur is stronger. It usually means that "I'll do it if I <u>absolutely</u> have to". Theoretically, *à la limite* is a little milder and means something more like "I don't really want to but I'll do it if necessary". In practice though, it's hard to tell them apart and you can use them pretty interchangeably. For example:

Je pourrais le faire, à la rigueur.

I would be able to do it, if necessary.

À la rigueur, on peut trouver une autre solution.

In a pinch, we can find another solution.

C'est infect ! À la limite, je préfère ne rien manger que manger ça.

It's awful. If it comes to that, I'd rather eat nothing than eat that.

Tu parles !

The exclamation *Tu parles !* is very interesting because it can have two almost opposite meanings. Normally, it is a sign of agreement, and means something like: Dont I know it! You're telling me! You are right on! I agree!

S'il continue comme ça il va avoir des ennuis. --- Tu parles !

If he continues like that, he's going to have problems. --- That's for sure!

Ah ! C'est une jolie fille. --- Tu parles !

Oh! She is a pretty girl. --- I agree! Don't I know it!

However, sometimes *Tu parles !* is said ironically and with a deprecatory tone of voice and means pretty much the opposite, something like: You've got to be kidding! You must be joking! You don't know what you're talking about!

Naturally, you should be able to tell by the tone of voice and the context.

> *Je crois qu'ils vont gagner la Coupe du monde.*
> *--- Oh, tu parles!*

> I think that they will win the World Cup. ---
> Oh, don't be silly!

Et alors ?

Et alors ? literally means "And then?" and is used to say something like: And so? And what of it? So what?

> *Les voisins peuvent nous voir. --- Et alors?*

> But the neighbors can see us. --- So what!
> What of it?

Sometimes it's said with a touch a futility to say "There's not much we can do about it", or "What can we do about it?".

> *Il est possible qu'ils aient triché. --- Et alors?*
> (With a shrug of the shoulders).

> It's possible that they cheated. --- So, what
> can we do about it?

In other contexts *Et alors* can be said aggressively, as a challenge.

> *Vous dansez avec ma copine. --- Et alors ?*

You're dancing with my girlfriend! --- And so, what are you going to do about it?

Tu n'as pas encore fait la vaisselle ! --- Et alors ?

You haven't yet done the dishes! --- So what's the big deal?

au juste ?

Au juste means "exactly". It's added to a question to request the person responding to be precise, (or more precise). This means that you can use it, and may hear it, in a multitude of circumstances. For example:

C'est où dans Paris, au juste ?

It's where in Paris, exactly?

Quand est-ce que vous allez venir, au juste?

When exactly are you going to arrive?

Ils étaient combien à la réunion, au juste ?

There were how many at the meeting exactly?

Ça coûte combien, au juste ?

How much exactly does that cost?

Tu me dis de venir. Mais quand, au juste ?

You say I should come. But *when*, exactly?

Ça c'est quoi, au juste ?

What is that, exactly?

Remember that au juste is used with the question words *quand, combien, quoi,* and *où.*

avoir l'habitude de
prendre l'habitude de
perdre l'habitude de

These three expressions mean: to have the habit of, to get in the habit of, to lose the habit of. As with most of the expressions in this book, they aren't restricted to any one circumstance but are very versatile.

They could also be translated: to be used to, to get used to, to no longer be used to. For example:

J'ai l'habitude de me coucher tard.

> I'm in the habit of going to bed late / I'm used to going to bed late.

J'ai pris l'habitude de me coucher tard quand j'étais étudiant.

> I got in the habit of going to bed late when I was a student.

Maintenant j'ai perdu l'habitude de me coucher tard.

> Now I've lost the habit of going to bed late.

56

J'ai l'habitude du froid.

I'm used to cold weather.

J'ai l'habitude d'étudier pendant des heures.

I'm used to studying a lot.

Nous avons perdu l'habitude de boire du vin pendant le repas.

We've gotten out of the habit of drinking wine with meals.

We're no longer used to drinking wine with meals.

dès que
sitôt

Dès que (the "s" is not pronounced), means "as soon as". You can use *dès que* whenever you would say "as soon as" in English.

Il a commencé à travailler dès qu'il est arrivé.

He started to work as soon as he arrived.

Dès qu'il l'a vue, il a souri.

As soon as he saw her he smiled.

Another word meaning "as soon as" is *sitôt*. *Sitôt* is much less frequently used than *dès que*.

Il a commencé à travailler sitôt qu'il est ar-rivé.

Sitôt arrivé, il a commencé à travailler.

en

The pronoun *en* can mean: of it, of them, from it, from them, by it, because of it, or with it. It **refers back** to something, or some things, already mentioned.

En has no counterpart in English but it is much used in spoken (and in written) French. I'm giving you a lot of examples to show some of the many different ways *en* is used:

Avez-vous des melons ? --- Combien en voulez-vous ? --- J'en veux quatre.

Do you have melons? --- How many <u>of them</u> do you want? --- I'd like four <u>of them</u>.

Because it has no counterpart in English, English speakers tend to omit the *en* when speaking French. In the sentence above, they might just say *"Je veux quatre"* instead of *"J'en veux quatre"*. Unfortunately, however, *"Je veux quatre"* is incorrect and sounds incorrect to a francophone.

J'en étais bouleversé.

I was shaken <u>by it</u>.

J'en ai trois.

I have three <u>of them</u>.

Elle n'en dort plus la nuit.

She doesn't sleep any more at night <u>because</u> <u>of it</u>.

Est-ce qu'il a encore la grippe. --- Non. Il en est guéri.

Does he still have the flu. --- No. He is cured <u>of it</u>.

Combien il y en a ? --- Il y en a six.

How many <u>of them</u> are there? --- There are six <u>of them</u>.

J'en ai eu assez.

I have had enough <u>of it</u> or <u>of them</u>. (When eating, for example).

Avez-vous besoin d'essence? ---- J'en ai assez.

Do you need gasoline? --- I have enough <u>of</u> <u>it</u>.

Est-ce qu'il y a beaucoup de voitures sur cette route ? ---Il y en a trop.

Are there a lot of cars on that route? --- There are too many (<u>of them</u>).

Just remember to drop the *en* into your sentence when you are referring back to something which has already been mentioned. Here are a few more examples. Practice putting in the translations yourself.

Quand Jean-Michel en aura fini...

Où puis-je trouver un boucher ? --- Il y en a un rue Florentin.

Il en était convaincu.

Elle avait besoin d'une robe de soir. Elle m'a demandé s'il était vrai que j'en louais.

au fur et à mesure

The expression *au fur et à mesure* means something pretty close "as one goes along". It's used for something that you do in little bits, as you go.

Nous en discuterons au fur et à mesure durant notre promenade.

We will discuss it (a bit at a time) as we go along during our walk.

Vous allez apprendre à parler le français, et vous apprendrez la grammaire au fur et à mesure.

You'll learn to speak French and you'll learn the grammar as you go along.

Regardez ces dessins et passez-les moi au fur et à mesure.

Look at these drawings and pass them to me as you go.

gêner

Gêner is a verb that means "to be in the way", "to block", "to disturb", or "to interfere", when discussing an action. For example:

(On a curbside sign) *Stationnement gênant.*

> Parking here is in the way, interferes with traffic. (The sign may have a little picture of a tow truck for emphasis).

Cet arbre gêne la vue.

> That tree blocks the view.

However, the expression that is important for you to learn is a little expression of *politesse* (politeness). You use it to politely ask permission to do something.

Ça te gênes si je....? or

Est-ce que ça te gênes si je....?.

> Will it bother you if I...?

Ça te gênes si j'allume la télévision?

> Will it bother you if I put on the television.

And more formally:

Est-ce que cela vous gênerait si nous venions un peu plus tard / tôt ?

Would it bother you (be a problem for you) if we arrive a bit later / earlier?

A second meaning for the verb *gêner* is to embarrass or make to feel awkward:

Elle était gênée de le rencontrer encore une fois.

She was embarrassed (she felt awkward) to run into him once again.

Il était un peu gênant de faire l'amour quand mes parents étaient dans la maison.

It was a little embarrassing / awkward to make love with my parents in the house.

This brings us to another expression that I'll throw in for free: *sans-gêne*. Literally *sans-gêne* means "without embarrassment". In practice it can best be translated as: without shame, shameless, impudent, brazen.

Oh ! Il est sans gêne !

Oh! He's shameless!

chouette

Chouette (pronounced "shwette"), is a colloquial expression of approval, meaning, depending on context: excellent, great, beautiful, pretty, agreeable, attractive, or *"sympa"*.

Chouette expresses enthusiasm and is usually said with enthusiasm and gusto. It's most often used by young people but, as with many youthful expressions, it has spread throughout the population.

C'est chouette !

It's super!

Je t'invite pour demain soir. --- Chouette!

I'm inviting you for tomorrow night. --- Swell! great!

C'est une chemise très chouette.

It's a really beautiful shirt.

C'est un chouette type.

He's very "sympa".

Elle était très chouette avec nous.

She was very nice and likeable with us.

C'était une chouette balade.

It was a very nice walk.

Maman me manque quand elle part en voyage mais en même temps c'est chouette parce que je fait plein de trucs avec papa que maman n'aimerait pas.

I miss Mommy when she's on a trip but at the same time it's neat because I do a lot of things with Daddy that Mommy wouldn't like. (Paraphrased from *Lignes de faille* by Nancy Huston)

By the way, the noun *une chouette* is an owl, and is not immediately related to the adjective *chouette* that you just learned.

chic

Chic, which ordinarily means elegant, can be used in casual language in the same way as *chouette*, meaning "excellent" or *"sympa"*.

> *C'est un très chic type.*
>
> > He's very "sympa".
>
> *Marie est une chic fille.*
>
> > Marie is a neat girl.
>
> *Elle a été très chic avec nous.*
>
> > She has been very nice (sympa) with us.

Chic ! can also be used as an exclamation in the same way as *Chouette !*

> *Je t'invite pour demain soir. --- Chic alors!*
>
> > I'm inviting you for tomorrow evening. --- Great!

My daughter tells me she would use *Chic !* more often than *Chouette !* to accept an invitation. You can also just say *Oui, avec plasir! C'est une bonne idée !* or *D'accord, merci.*

Génial !

Génial ! is another expression like *chouette* and *chic*, which means "Terrific!" or "Great idea!" in casual speech.

On peut y aller demain. --- Génial !

We can go tomorrow. --- Great idea!

en avoir marre

The expression *en avoir marre* is a strong expression which means "to be fed up (with it)". It's usually used as *j'en ai marre*. It's certainly an expression that you may have need of from time to time. For example: *J'en ai marre d'étudier le français !*

It would be possible to say *nous en avons marre* or *ils en ont marre*, meaning "we are fed up" or "they are fed up", but you'll hear these less frequently.

We recently discussed the use of *en* as a pronoun. *J'en ai marre* is another example of its use.

J'en ai marre ! or J'en ai marre de tout ça !

I'm fed up with that!

J'en ai marre de tes âneries !

I've had enough of your imbecilities!

There are several expressions in English which say the same thing as "I'm fed up with that", such as:

I've had enough of that.

I'm sick and tired of that.

I've had it up to here with that.

There are several synonymous expressions in French as well. For example:

J'en ai par-dessus la tête de ça.

I've had it up to here with that.
(literally "over my head")

Elle en a ras-le-bol de son boulot.

She's sick and tired of her job.
(literally "her bowl is full to the brim")

J'en ai assez de ses caprices.

I've had enough of her tantrums / whims.

J'ai plein le dos de ses caprices.
(literally, "my back is loaded down with" or "I have a full load of")

Ça suffit ! Trop c'est trop !

That's enough! Too much is too much!

These are all pretty much equivalent expressions and you can use whichever you like interchangeably. *J'en ai marre* and *Ça suffit* are probably the ones you'll hear the most often, however.

je m'en fiche
je m'en fous
je m'en balance
je me moque

This brings us to *je m'en fiche* which means in essence: "I don't care a hoot about it" or "I couldn't care less about it" or "I don't give a damn about it". *Je m'en fiche* is often said a bit scornfully.

If you refer to a particular thing that you don't care about, you no longer need the *en* and you drop it. You therefore say *je me fiche de (quelque chose)* as in:

> *Je m'en fiche / Je me fiche de ça.*
>
>> I don't care about that. I couldn't care less about it.
>
> *Je me fiche de ses problèmes.*
>
>> I don't care about his problems.
>
> *Je me fiche de la politique / La politique, je m'en fiche.*
>
>> I don't give a darn about politics. (In the second sentence you are referring back to *la politique* so you say *je m'en fiche*.)

Je m'en fiche is of course from casual spoken language. You will hear it used frequently.

There are several other expressions which mean about the same thing as *je m'en fiche*. For example, *Je m'en fous and je m'en balance* are also from casual spoken language and have the same meaning.

On the other hand, *je me moque de ça* is more refined and literary French, while also meaning the same thing. However *se moquer de* can also mean to make fun of or to mock and you may be misunderstood if you don't use it correctly.

It's thus probably safer to stick with *je m'en fiche* in ordinary conversation. *The verb ficher* also has different meanings, but the meanings of *je m'en fiche* and *je me fiche de ça* are clear and unambiguous.

Ça m'est égal.

Je m'en fiche is a strong statement meaning "I don't give a damn". If you just want to say that you don't care one way or another about a subject or a decision, you can use *ça m'est égal* which means "it's all the same to me". *Ça m'est égal* is proper French while *je m'en fiche* is more casual French.

> *Qu'est-ce que tu préfères, aller à la pizzeria ou au restaurant chinois ce soir ? --- Ça m'est égal.*

> Which would you prefer, to go to the piz-

zeria or to the Chinese restaurant this evening? --- It's all the same to me.

soi

The prounoun *soi* means "oneself" (or, if you are talking
about a particular person, "himself" or "herself"). It can
be used in a number of useful expressions and our discussion of *soi* will be followed by a stream of derivative
expressions. Let's start with *soi,* itself:

> *Il est bon de rentrer chez soi quand on est fa-
> tigué.*
>
> > It's good to return to one's home when one
> > is tired.
>
> *Il faut rester maître de soi.*
>
> > It's important to keep one's self control.
> >
> > It's necessary to stay in control of oneself.
> >
> > It's necessary to remain master of oneself.
>
> *Il faut avoir confiance en soi.*
>
> > It's necessary to have confidence in oneself.
>
> *C'est chacun pour soi.*
>
> > It's every man for himself.

en soi

En soi can be translated by "in itself" or "intrinsically" or "by it's very nature" or "by itself". For example:

> *C'est suffisant en soi.*
>
> > That's sufficient in itself / by itself.
>
> *Cette loi n'est pas mauvaise en soi, mais son application n'est pas facile.*
>
> > That law isn't bad in itself, but to apply it is not easy.
>
> *Cette épreuve, en soi, était accablante.*
>
> > That ordeal, in itself, was overwhelming.

soi-disant

Literally, *soi-disant* means "self-saying" or "self-claiming". As an adjective it refers usually to a person, and would be translated as "self-styled" or "so-called". It implies skepticism on the speakers part. A French synonym would be *prétendu*.

For example:

> *Ce soi-disant plombier n'y connaît rien en plomberie.*
>
> > That self-styled plumber knows nothing about plumbing.

Soi-disant can also refer to something which isn't what it's claimed to be, in which case it's translated as "so-called".

> *La soi-disant princesse...*
>
> > The self-proclaimed / so called princess.
>
> *Sous la dictature, le soi-disant système de lois n'était qu'illusion.*
>
> > Under the dictatorship the so called system of law was only an illusion.

cela va de soi

Literally, *cela va de soi,* or *ça va de soi* means "that goes by itself". It can be translated as "that's self evident", or "that goes without saying".

> *Ça va de soi que nous allons payer les frais.*
>
> > It goes without saying that we are going to pay the expenses.
>
> *Ça va de soi !*
>
> > That goes without saying! Of course!
>
> *Cela ne va pas de soi.*
>
> > That's not self-evident at all ("and I'm not at all sure it's true").

soi-même

Our final expression using *soi*, *soi-même* means "one-self".

> *Dans ce gîte, on doit faire le ménage soi-même.*

> In that rental cottage one has to do the housekeeping oneself.

> *C'est très difficile de se juger soi-même.*

> It's very difficult to evaluate oneself.

> *On a du mal à se chatouiller soi-même.*

> It's difficult to tickle yourself.

peu importe

The French verb *importer* has two meanings. The first is familiar to us. *Importer* can mean "to import" (goods into the country).

The second meaning though, is "to matter" or "to have importance".

(This is where the English adjective "important" comes from. It's the present participle of *importer,* and, therefore, means "mattering" or "having importance").

Thus *peu importe* means "it's of little importance" or "it matters little". For example:

Pierre ne peut pas venir à la réunion. -- Peu importe.

Pierre can't come to the meeting. --- It matters little. It doesn't matter.

Peu importe qu'il vienne ou pas.

It's of little importance if he comes or not.

Est-ce que tu préfères manger dans un restaurant chinois ou italien ? --- Peu importe.

Do you prefer to eat at a Chinese restaurant or an Italian? --- It's of little importance.

n'importe

N'importe is a very similar expression but it isn't exactly the same. It means "no matter" or "it doesn't matter". For example:

Tu peux venir à n'importe quelle heure. Je serai à la maison toute la journée.

You can come at no matter what time (whenever you like). I'll be at the house all day.

Tu préfères lequel ? --- N'importe.

Which do you prefer? --- It's not important / It doesn't matter / Either one.

Vous pouvez le poser n'importe où.

You can put it down anywhere.

Tu fais n'importe quoi et tu crois que je vais l'accepter.

> You just do whatever you like and you think that I will accept it.

Pour moi, tu peux acheter n'importe quelle glace. J'aime tous les parfums.

> You can buy me whichever flavor of ice cream. I like them all.

Cela peut arriver n'importe quand à n'importe qui.

> That could happen to anyone, any time. (Literally "no matter when to no matter who").

Je n'y suis pour rien

The expression *Je n'y suis pour rien* is a denial. It means "I had nothing to do with it" or "It has nothing to do with me". For example, this quote from a *policier*:

Montale, j'y suis pour rien. Je te jure.

> Montale, I had nothing to do with it. I swear to you.

This expression could also be used in the second person or third person.

Les apparences sont contre lui, mais je crois qu'il n'y est pour rien.

The circumstances are against him but I believe that he has nothing to do with it.

Les apparences sont contre vous, mais je crois que vous n'y êtes pour rien.

The circumstances are against you but I believe that you have nothing to do with it.

enfin

The adverb *enfin* is a very common word which has a number of differently nuanced meanings.

1.   *Enfin* can mean "at least" in the following sense:

J'ai vu ton frère. Enfin, je pense que c'était lui.

I saw your brother. At least I think it was he.

C'est un vrai maître aux échecs. Enfin, il joue beaucoup mieux que moi.

He's a real chess master. At least he plays much better than me.

2.   *Enfin* can mean "finally" or "at last". For example:

Je vous ai enfin retrouvé.

I found you again at last.

Vous voilà ! Enfin !

There you are! Finally!

3.   *Enfin* can also mean "in brief" or "to sum up".
(French synonyms would be *bref,* or *en somme.*)

Il y avait chez moi ma mère, mon père, mes frères... enfin toute la famille.

> There were, at my house, my mother, my father, my brothers... in brief, the whole family.

Enfin, c'était de la folie.

> To sum up, it was craziness.

4.   *Enfin* can sometimes be used as a synonym for however or nevertheless (*cependant ou néanmoins*).

Je te déconseille de faire ça, enfin tu fais ce que tu veux.

> I advise you not to do that. However, you do what you want.

5.   Finally, *enfin* can express exasperation, as in:

Mais enfin ! Il ment ! C'est pas vrai !

> He's lying! It's not true!

Mais enfin, je vous l'avais déjà dit !

> But really! I already told you!

en effet
en fait, de fait
effectivement
réellement

The expression *en effet* means: indeed, actually, really, in actual fact. That's a lot of definitions for you to decipher but you'll understand better with a few examples:

Oui, j'étais là cet été, en effet.

Yes, I was there this summer, as a matter of fact.

Yes, I was really there this summer.

En effet je pensais la même chose.

Actually I was thinking the same thing.

The expressions *effectivement, réellement, en fait* and *de fait* mean pretty much the same thing as *en effet* : actually, as a matter of fact, in fact.

Oui, j'étais là cet été, effectivement.

Yes, I was there this summer, as a matter of fact.

Oui, j'étais là cet été, réellement.

Yes I was really there this summer.

En fait, je peux venir demain.

In fact, I can come tomorrow.

There is a small nuance of difference, however, between *en effet* and *en fait*. Look at the next three examples:

> *Il a estimé que ça allait coûter mille euros, et en effet c'était le prix exact.*

> > He estimated that it would cost a thousand euros, and actually that was the exact price.

> *Il a estimé que ça allait coûter mille euros. En fait ça a coûté mille cinq cents.*

> > He estimated that it would cost a thousand euros. In fact it cost fifteen hundred.

> *Il m'a dit que la maison était en bon état. En fait elle était délabrée.*

> > He told me the house was in good shape. In fact, it was dilapidated.

Note how *en effet* is used to confirm (that it was *mille euros*) while *en fait* (in fact) is used to contradict, to say that **in fact** it was different.

pendant que
tandis que

The expression *pendant que* means "while" in the sense of "during the time that".

> *Pendant qu'elle était à Paris, elle a visité le Louvre.*

While she was in Paris, she visited the Louvre. (During the time that...)

On the other hand, *tandis que* means "while" in the sense of "whereas". In other words, while one person (or thing) was doing or being something, another person (or thing) was doing or being something else. While things are occurring at the same time, there is a sense that they are **opposing** actions or states of being.

Il est riche, tandis que son frère est pauvre.

He's rich, while / whereas his brother is poor.

Son frère est resté chez eux, tandis qu'elle est venue à Paris.

Her brother stayed at home, while she came to Paris. (Make note of the difference between this and the Paris example above which used *pendant que*).

Son frère est paresseux, tandis qu'il est travailleur.

His brother is lazy, whereas he's a hard worker.

toujours
depuis toujours
pour toujours

Toujours means always.

Est-ce que tu m'aimeras toujours ?

Do you think that you will love me always?

Il a toujours vécu ici. / Il va toujours vivre ici.

He has always lived here. / He will always live
here.

If you make it *depuis toujours* it is literally "since always".
It puts it specifically in the past and provides emphasis.
Note the difference between:

J'ai toujours voulu un chat.

I've always wanted a cat.

J'ai voulu un chat depuis toujours.

I've wanted a cat forever / I've wanted a cat
all my life.

On the other hand, *pour toujours* literally is "for always"
and it sounds almost redundant to an English speaker. Using *pour* is usually used to specify a particular amount
of time as in *pour trois jours*, but in the case of *pour
toujours,* It anchors the sentence firmly in the future and
seems to be used for emphasis. It can be translated as
"forever" or "permanently" or "for good"."For good" actually probably fits best.

Elle est guérie pour toujours.

She is cured for good.

Elle va rester ici pour toujours.

She will stay here for good.

You can see from these two examples that the nuance of meaning of *pour toujours* is indeed different from that of a simple *toujours*, although the difference may be hard to put into precise words.

il n'empêche que
n'empêche

The verb *empêcher* means: to prevent, to hold back from doing, to impede.

When translated literally, *il n'empêche que...* says "it doesn't prevent that...".

Thus when used in a figurative sense, *il n'empêche que* means "nevertheless" or "even so".

> *Nous avons gagné la bataille. --- Il n'empêche que nous l'avons payé cher.*

> > We won the battle. --- Nevertheless we paid dearly.

> *Nous serons quatre à travailler. --- Il n'empêche que cela va être un gros boulot.*

> > There will be four of us working. --- Even so it will be a big job.

In very casual speech, the expression is often shortened to just *N'empêche*.

Nous serons quatre à travailler. --- N'empêche, c'est un gros boulot.

There will be four of us working. --- Even so, it's a big job.

N'empêche, tu aurais pu téléphoner.

Nevertheless, you could have telephoned.

Ne t'inquiète pas !
T'inquiète !

The adjective *inquiet* in French (literally "unquiet"), translates as worried, anxious, uneasy or unquiet.

While in English, we would not make unquiet or uneasy into a verb (to unquiet?), the French make *inquiet* into *inquiéter*. The verb *inquiéter* means, naturally enough, "to make uneasy or worried".

The reflexive form *s'inquiéter* thus means "to make yourself worried" or "to get worried" or "to worry yourself".

From which we finally arrive at the common expression *Ne t'inquiète pas !* which means: Don't worry yourself! Don't upset yourself! No big deal!

Ne t'inquiète pas ! Ce n'est pas important.

Don't worry, it's not important.

In casual spoken French, *Ne t'inquiète pas !* is often abbreviated to *T'inquiète pas !* and, most frequently, to just *T'inquiète !*

> *T'inquiète pas ! C'est pas important.*

> *T'inquiète ! C'est pas important.*

> Don't worry, it's not important.

Ne te fais pas de souci
Ne t'en fais pas
T'en fait pas
Pas de souci

The expression *ne te fais pas de souci* literally means "don't make worry for yourself", and it's pretty much a synonym for *ne t'inquiète pas.*

> *Ne te fais pas de souci ! Ce n'est pas important.*

> Don't worry, it's not important.

Ne te fais pas de souci is very often abbreviated as *Ne t'en fais pas* (where *en* takes the place of *de souci*), and even more often in casual speech as *T'en fais pas.*

> *Ne t'en fais pas ! Ce n'est pas important.*

> Don't worry, it's not important.

> *T'en fais pas ! C'est pas important.*

> Don't worry, it's not important.

Ne te fais pas de souci is also sometimes abbreviated using just the last three words *Pas de souci !* and means "No worry" in the sense of "No problem". We'll discuss *Pas de souci !* at greater length later on when we discuss *Pas de problème !*

> *Est-ce que tu peux faire ça pour moi ? --- Pas de souci !*

>> Can you do that for me? --- No worry/ No problem!

Ne te casse pas la tête !
Te casse pas la tête !

Ne te casse pas la tête is another similar expression. It literally means "Don't break your head", and can be translated as "Don't rack your brains" or "Don't worry about it, it's not important".

> *Je ne vois pas comment je pourrai venir demain. --- Ne te casse pas la tête ! Ce n'est pas important.*

>> I don't see how I can come tomorrow. --- Don't worry about it. It's not important.

In casual spoken French it's heard more commonly as *Te casse pas la tête !*

> *Je crois pas que je puisse venir demain. --- Te casse pas la tête. C'est pas important.*

I don't think I can come tomorrow. --- Don't worry about it. It's not important.

You must remember that expressions like *T'inquiète !* and *Te casse pas la tête !* from spoken French, are not standard French. When you are in a situation when standard French is expected, you must use the proper longer forms.

The French almost all use the casual forms in everyday speech, but expect standard French in more formal situations. This even carries over to written French, where someone writing a casual note to a friend may well use a short form, in a business letter he or she will certainly use the standard long form.

I don't mean to confuse you with these expressions from casual speech. I include them because that's the way people talk, and this book is about spoken French and everyday expressions.

embêtant
Tu m'embêtes !

The verb *embêter* means: to irritate, bother or annoy. *Embêtant* is "annoying".

Tu es très embêtant !

You are very annoying.

Finally we have the common expression:

Tu m'embêtes !

You are really getting on my nerves.

The context where these would be used are a mother to an annoying child, a sibling to another, one roommate or friend to another, one spouse to another. (It can be used as a semi-pleasantry and usually doesn't express serious anger).

Emmerdant and *chiant* are vulgar and slangy equivalents to *embêtant*. I am including them so that you will recognize them but I would advise you against using *emmerdant* or *chiant* in conversation. One has to be very familiar with both the language and social customs to be sure of not offending.

Attention !
fais attention
fais gaffe

Attention ! means "Watch out!" or "Be careful!" and is obviously useful to know.

You use *"Fais attention"* when you are telling someone to watch out or to be careful around a particular thing or person. (It's *"Faites attention"*, of course, if you are using the *vous* form to address the person or persons you are talking to).

Fais attention ! C'est un manipulateur.

Watch out! / Be careful! He's a manipulator.

Faites attention si vous passez par là pendant la nuit.

Watch out if you go past there at night.

Fais attention à ses dents.

Watch out for her teeth (referring to a dog).

Fais attention à toi quand tu vas skier.

Be careful of yourself when you go skiing.

Fais attention. Tu vas tomber !

Watch out, you are going to fall!

A synonym of *Fais attention* is *Fais gaffe.*

Fais gaffe. Tu vas tomber !

Watch out, you are going to fall!

Be careful, you'll fall.

This is a bit of an an odd idiom since *une gaffe* is a boat hook, or in casual language, a blunder. Nonetheless, *fais gaffe !* means watch out!

prêter attention à

On the other hand, *prêter attention à* means "to pay attention to". It's easy to confuse with *faire attention* which we just discussed, but it doesn't mean the same thing.

Prête attention à ta mère !

Pay attention to your mother!

Prêtez attention à ses conseils. C'est une femme sensée.

Pay attention to her advice. She's a sensible woman.

Gare à toi !

Gare à toi also means "Watch out!" However, while *Attention !* or *Faites attention !* is usually a well intentioned alerting, *Gare à toi !* often means "Watch out!" in the sense of a menace, as in:

Gare à toi si tu fais ça encore une fois!

You better watch out if you do that again!

In other cases *Gare à...* can mean "watch out for", just like *Attention à...*

Gare à cette marche qui n'est pas bien fixée.

Watch out for that loose step.

Gare à Jean-Luc !

Watch out for Jean-Luc!

voilà

In general, *voilà* means "there is" as in

Voilà ma maison !

There's my house!

Voilà Jean !

There's Jean!

Le voilà ! means "There he is!" or "There it is!" but it can also mean "Here he is!" or "Here it is!"

La voilà !

Here she is!

Me voilà !

Here I am!

(Notice that you use the direct objects *Le, La* or *Me* and not the subjects *Il, Elle* or *Je*, with these expressions).

Next I have four expressions which you are more likely to encounter in reading rather than in conversation, but which can be very confusing. They are *quitte à, avoir beau, se garder de faire*, and *qui fait.*

quitte à

The expression *quitte à* has the sense "even if it means" or "even at the risk of". The expression is built with the verb after *quitte à* in the infinitive.

Starting from *"quitte à"*, this meaning is very unintuitive for an English speaker, so you may be led astray. Here are some examples:

Je finirai ce travail, quitte à revenir demain matin.

I'll finish the job, even if it means coming back tomorrow morning.

Je resterai jusqu'au bout avec toi, quitte à mourir ensemble.

I'll stay to the end with you, even if it means dying together.

avoir beau

The expression *avoir beau* is another very unintuitive little idiom. *Avoir beau* means: even though, inspite of, no matter how hard. (A French synonym would be *bien que* but the sentence structure is different as you will see).

Avoir beau is usually used in the form: *"J'ai beau (with the verb in the **infinitive**), je (with the second verb in the **present** tense)"*.

Here are some examples:

J'ai beau essayer, je n'y arrive pas.

Even though I try / Inspite of trying / No matter how hard I try, I don't succeed.

Elle a beau lui expliquer, il ne comprend pas.

Even though she explains, he doesn't understand.

Il a beau le lui dire, elle ne veut rien entendre.

No matter how hard he tries to tell her, she just won't listen.

Even though he tells her, she doesn't want to hear.

Even though the expression starts with a *"j'ai"* or an *"il a"* you actually do use it with the infinitive instead of the past participle, and you do translate it in the present tense. It's very peculiar, but that's the way it is.

If you want to use *avoir beau* in the past you'd say: *"j'avais beau... (keeping the verb in the infinitive), je... (with the second verb in the imparfait)"*.

J'avais beau essayer, je le ratais à chaque fois.

Even though I tried/ Inspite of having tried / No matter how hard I tried, I failed every time.

Elle avait beau lui expliquer, il ne comprenait pas.

Even though she explained, he didn't understand.

Il avait beau se dire qu'elle allait venir, il savait bien que ce n'était pas le cas.

No matter how hard he told himself that she would come, he was well aware that it wouldn't happen.

se garder de (faire quelque chose)

The expression *se garder de*, when followed by an infinitive, means "to be careful not to do". Although it expresses a negative, you do not have to include a *ne...pas* with the verb that comes after it to make it negative. For example:

> *Il s'est bien gardé de donner la vraie raison de sa visite.*
>
>> He was very careful **not** to give the true reason for his visit.

> *Il se garde de manger les huîtres crues.*
>
>> He is careful **not** to eat raw oysters.

> *Il se garde bien de déposer tout son argent à la banque.*
>
>> He is careful **not** to deposit all his money at the bank.

> *Je m'en garderai bien.*
>
>> I'll be careful **not** to do that. / Don't worry! No way I'll do that!

> *Gardez-vous, leur dit-il, de vendre l'héritage. (La Fontaine)*
>
>> Be careful, he told them, **not** to sell the heritage.

Note that, on the other hand, when the expression *se*

garder de is followed by the name of a food, instead of a verb, it means "to keep well". For example:

> *Le poisson se garde au réfrigérateur.*

> Fish keeps well in the refrigerator.

> *Les ailes de raie ne se gardent pas bien. Elles sont fragiles.*

> Skate wings don't keep well. They're fragile (and spoil easily).

Also when *se garder* de is followed by a person or a thing it means "watch out for..." or "don't trust..." or "be on the guard for..." For example:

> *Il faut se garder des flatteurs .*

> *Garde-toi de Philippe.*

qui fait (quelque chose)

This expression isn't quite so unintuitive. It refers to someone or something who is in the act of, or in the process of, doing something. It can be used with any verb, not just with *faire*.

It's the sentence structure, which is unusual for us anglophones, which makes *qui fait* idiomatic for us.

> *Je l'entends dans la cuisine, qui fait le petit déjeuner.*

I hear him in the kitchen, in the act of making breakfast.

Je l'ai vu dans sa chambre, qui étudiait fort.

I saw her in her room, in the act of studying hard / in the process of studying hard.

J'ai vu Jean dans sa chambre, qui se reposait enfin.

I saw Jean in his room, in the process of resting at long last.

I have heard each of these last four idioms used in spoken language, but as I have said, you are more likely to encounter them in reading than in speech.

en fin de compte
tout compte fait
au bout de compte

The expression *en fin de compte* is translated as "when you sum it all up" or "to conclude" or "in conclusion". Although *en fin de compte* is similar to the expression *enfin* which was discussed earlier, and could possibly be used as a synonym for it, *en fin de compte* is stronger and more encompassing than *enfin*.

Enfin is usually used just to sum up the speakers words as in:

Il y avait ma mère, mes frères... enfin toute la famille.

Enfin, c'était stupide.

En fin de compte, on the other hand, is more likely to be used after a discussion to sum up what has been decided. It expresses a conclusion. For example:

(after a discussion) - *En fin de compte, il paraît que nous avons un grave problème ici.*

To sum up, it appears that we have a serious problem here.

If you compare the above examples, the difference in usage between *enfin* and *en fin de compte* should become clear.

Tout compte fait and *au bout de compte* are synonyms of *en fin de compte.*

Tout compte fait, il paraît que nous avons un grave problème ici.

Au bout de compte, il paraît que nous avons un grave problème ici.

vos coordonnées

You will frequently be asked for your *coordonées,* which means your address, phone number, email address, etc.

Donnez-moi vos coordonnées s'il vous plaît.

Give me your address and phone number, please.

> *Est-ce que vous pouvez me donnez vos coor-*
> *données?*

> Can you give me your address and phone
> number?

par la suite
ensuite

While the **adjective** "next" is translated by *prochain* or
suivant, as in *la semaine prochaine*, the **adverb** "next"
can be translated by *par la suite* as in:

> *Et qu'est-ce qu'ils ont fait par la suite ?*

> And what did they do next?

> *Qu'est-ce que je dois faire par la suite ?*

> What should I do next?

> *Par la suite, j'ai rendu visite à Jean.*

> Next, I visited Jean.

Other terms that you can use for the same purpose are
ensuite and *après cela*. For example:

> *Ensuite, j'ai rendu visite à Jean.*

> *Après cela j'ai rendu visite à Jean.*

tout à l'heure

The expression *tout à l'heure* is rather unique as it can

mean either "a little while ago" or "in a little while". *Tout à l'heure* is a very common expression:

> *À tout à l'heure !*
>
>> I'll see you in a little while.
>
> *Il est arrivé tout à l'heure.*
>
>> He arrived a couple of minutes ago.
>
> *Je vais rentrer tout à l'heure.*
>
>> I'll be back in a few minutes.

Ça m'étonnerait (que)

As you know, I've been attempting to give you expressions which are not resticted to one specific circumstance but which can be used every day, or nearly every day. *Ça m'étonnerait que...* is one of those expressions. It can be translated as "It would surprise me if" or "I'd be surprised if". You can be surprised about anything you want.

Surprendre is the verb which is closest in stem to "to surprise" and *étonner* is closer to "to astonish", but you will almost never hear *Ça me surprendrait* to mean "That would surprise me" In normal usage. It's place has been taken by *Ça m'étonnerait*.

> *Ça m'étonnerait qu'elle arrive demain.*
>
>> It would surprise me if she comes tomorrow.

I'd be surprised if she comes tomorrow.

Ça m'étonnerait qu'elle soit une vraie blonde.

It would surprise me if she's really a blond.

Je peux le faire. --- Ça m'étonnerait !!!!

I can do it. --- That would surprise me! (ironic)

The negative of this expression, *Ça ne m'étonnerait pas*, is also commonly used to say "It wouldn't surprise me", as in:

Ça m'étonnerait pas qu'elle ait beaucoup souffert avec ce mari là.

I wouldn't be surprised if she has suffered a lot with that husband of hers.

Ça ne m'étonnerait pas qu'elle arrive demain.

It wouldn't surprise me if she comes tomorrow.

I wouldn't be surprised if she comes tomorrow.

Just as in English, putting the negative on the second verb instead of on *étonnerait* changes the meaning.

Ça m'étonnerait qu'elle n'arrive pas demain.

It would surprise me if she doesn't come tomorrow.

The expression can also be used in the simple present tense as in:

Elle n'est pas ici ? Ça m'étonne.

She's not here? That surprises me.

Ça ne m'étonne pas vraiment.

That doesn't really surprise me.

je n'en reviens pas

Word-for-word, *je n'en reviens pas* means something like "I am not coming back to it" or "I'm not coming back from it". However, **the actual translation** is "I can't get over it" when you are emotionally moved, and "I can't believe it" when you are astonished.

Here are some examples:

Je n'en reviens pas qu'il soit mort.

I can't get over it that he's dead.

Il n'en revenait pas.

He didn't get over it.

Je n'en reviens toujours pas, tu sais, murmura Harry, l'oeil embué de larmes.

I still can't get over it, you know, murmured Harry, his eyes filling with tears.

Elle n'en revient pas de l'avoir vu si malade.

She can't get over having seen him so sick.

Nous avons vraiment réussi ? Je n'en reviens pas !

We really did it? I'm astonished!

We really did it? I can't believe it!

ainsi que

The word *ainsi* means "thus" as in:

Ainsi a fini notre troisième journée sur l'île.

and the two words *ainsi* and *que*, when put together, can mean "thus that" as in:

C'est ainsi qu'elle est arrivée ici.

It is thus that she arrived here.

C'est ainsi que se termine ce roman, avec...

It's thus that this novel ends, with...

However *ainsi que* together, as an expression, means "as well as". (It can also simply mean "as". It's not logical at all. You just have to remember it, although you can usually tell from context. Seeing *ainsi que* in a couple of sentences will help).

Je le connais déjà, ainsi que son frère.

I know him already, and his brother as well.

Il peut parler anglais et allemand ainsi que français.

He can speak English and German as well as French.

Ils élèvent des chèvres ainsi que des brebis.

They raise goats as well as sheep.

Ainsi que j'ai déjà expliqué...

As I have already explained...

franchement

Franchement is another useful multi-purpose word. Most commonly, *franchement* means: frankly, openly, sincerely, honestly. Here are some examples:

Je te dis franchement ce que j'en pense.

I'm telling you frankly what I think about it.

Franchement, je ne sais pas quoi faire.

Frankly, I don't know what to do.

Je vais te parler franchement.

I'm going to speak frankly.

As an exclamation, *Franchement !* expresses impatience or annoyance. It still means "frankly speaking" but can also be translated as "Really, now!" or something similar, as in:

Franchement ! Tu exagères !

Really now! You are going too far!

Tu es bête, franchement !

You are really stupid!

You are stupid, to speak frankly!

Franchement should not be confused with *forcément* or *vachement* which will be the next two terms I'll discuss.

forcément

The word *forcément* literally means "forcedly", and in practice can be translated by: of course, inevitably, necessarily, obviously, or obligatorily. Consider the following:

Il y avait un gros bouchon sur la route et nous étions forcément en retard.

There was a large traffic jam on the road and we were, of course, late.

Elle sera forcément triste quand elle entendra les nouvelles.

She will inevitably be sad when she hears the news.

When used by itself as an exclamation, *Forcément !* means "Of course!" A French synonym would be *Bien sûr !*

Tu seras là demain ? --- Forcément !

You'll be there tomorrow? --- Of course!
(Bien sûr !)

Finally, *pas forcément* means "not necessarily", as in:

Ce n'est pas forcément une très bonne idée.

That's not necessarily a great idea.

vachement

The adverb *vachement* is very slangy and not to be used at all in formal situations. It is used to intensify and means "to a very high degree". It has nothing to do with a cow (*une vache*).

Vachement can thus be translated as "fantastically" or "damned" or "very". French synonyms would be *drôlement* or *rudement*. *Vachement* is usually a positive, admiring expression as in:

Elle a vachement bien réussi.

She has succeeded fantastically well.

C'est vachement bien.

It's damned good.

La soupe est vachement bonne.

The soup is fantastically delicious.

However, occasionally *vachement* will accentuate a negative as in:

Il pleut vachement.

It's raining awfully hard.

Je suis vachement embêté.

I'm really bothered. (I can't find the answer to the problem).

Il est vachement con.

He is damned stupid.

You can almost always tell whether it is accentuating the positive or the negative from context.

à l'insu de

The expression *à l'insu de* means "without the knowledge of". It's another nice expression which can be used in many situations.

Il a acheté ça à l'insu de sa femme.

He bought that without his wife's knowledge.

Elle l'a fait à l'insu de Jean.

She did it without Jean's knowledge / behind Jean's back.

à mon insu

without my knowledge / behind my back

à son insu

without his (her) knowledge

à leur insu, à notre insu

When I first encountered *à l'insu de* I thought that it was a very peculiar expression which made no sense. Since, I have realized that *su* is the past participle of *savoir* (to know), and that therefore, as an adjective *su* means "known". As a noun *le su* is "the knowledge". Thus *l'insu* is "the lack of knowledge"! It's used only in this expression.

étant donné que

Étant donné que is a very useful and easy to remember expression. Word-for-word it means "being given that", and "given that" is exactly what it actually means.

You could also translate *étant donné que* as "considering that" or "in view of" or even simply as "since" or "because". It's used to say that in light of one thing happening, another is considered or possible. It's used in expressions like:

Étant donné que tu as fais un long voyage et que tu es très fatigué, nous devrions peut-être rester chez nous ce soir.

Given that you have travelled a lot, and are very tired, maybe we should stay home tonight.

Étant donné qu'on ne peut pas réserver, il est préférable d'arriver tôt.

> Given that we can't make a reservation, it will be better to arrive early.

Étant donné qu'il n'est pas arrivé, il faut modifier notre plan.

> Since he hasn't arrived, we have to change our plan.

Étant donné que le vol est annulé, nous devons nous y rendre en voiture.

> Given that the flight is cancelled, we have to get there by car.

Étant donné qu'il travaille à la mairie, il doit être au courant.

> Given that / Since he works at the town hall, he should know.

You can reverse the order of the sentence without any problem:

Il doit être au courant, étant donné qu'il travaille à la mairie.

> He ought to know, since / given that he works at the town hall.

Étant donné que gives you one of those rare chances to use an expression which sounds right in English and, amazingly, sounds just right in French as well.

106

puisque

Puisque means "since" or "seeing that" and thus, is a synonym for *étant donné que* :

> *Puisqu'il travaille à la mairie, il doit être au courant.*

Another synonym for *étant donné que* is *du moment que*.

> *Elle est heureuse, du moment qu'il y a beaucoup à manger.*

> She's happy, given that there's plenty to eat.

Note that in English, we use the same word, "since", for two entirely different meanings, which are translated differently in French.

The **first** meaning for "since" in English is "given that" or "because". This sense is translated in French by *étant donné que*, by *puisque,* or by *du moment où.*

> *Étant donné que l'avion est en retard...*

> Since the plane is late...

The **second** meaning of "since" in English refers to an intervening period of time, and is translated in French by *depuis.*

> *Je ne l'ai pas vu depuis que je suis arrivé.*

> I haven't seen him since I arrived.

If you think about it, you will realize that these two different meanings for the word "since" that we have in English are not related to each other at all.

du moment que
compte tenu de
vu que
parce que
comme

This is a group of French expressions which all can mean roughly about the same thing as *étant donné que* and *puisque*.

Du moment que is used not infrequently. However, *du moment que* is such an unintuitive way to say "given that" that you are less likely to actually use it yourself. It would be useful to be able to recognize it, though, as you will certainly encounter it in reading.

The other French expressions with about the same meaning are *compte tenu de / que* (taking into account that), *vu que* (seeing that), *comme* (as), and *parce que* (because).

Du moment qu'il n'est pas arrivé, il faut modifier notre plan.

Compte tenu qu'il n'est pas arrivé, il faut...

Vu qu'il n'est pas arrivé, il faut...

Parce qu'il n'est pas arrivé, il faut...

Comme il n'est pas arrivé, il faut...

Compte tenu de l'annulation du vol, nous dev-
ons nous y rendre en voiture.

d'après...
selon

The expression *d'après* is very simple. It means "accord-ing to", as in:

D'après Jean, il va neiger demain.

According to Jean it's going to snow tomor-row.

D'après Marie Claire, Evelyne va arriver à l'aéroport à cinq heures.

According to Marie Claire, Evelyne will ar-rive at the airport at five o'clock.

You can reverse the order without problem:

Il va neiger demain d'après Jean.

It's going to snow tomorrow according to Jean.

A French synonym for *d'après* is *selon:*

Selon Jean il va neiger demain.

être pris

Literally, *je suis pris* means "I am taken", and it's the term you use when you are invited out, but you already have plans:

Oh, dommage! Je suis pris samedi soir.

Oh, what a shame! I'm busy Saturday evening.

Je suis désolé, mais nous sommes pris mardi. Est-ce que jeudi vous convient?

I'm very sorry, but we already have plans for Tuesday. Would Thursday work for you?

tenir pour acquis

The expression *tenir pour acquis* means "to take or to consider as already established". You could also translate it as "to take for granted". You can use it whenever you would say that something was taken for granted.

Il a tenu pour acquis qu'il allait gagner. C'était une grave erreur.

He took it for granted that he was going to win. It was a serious error.

Il a tenu les premiers trois axiomes pour acquis.

He considered the first three axioms as already established and not needing proof.

It's the word *acquis* that counts. If you forget *tenir pour acquis* you can say *considéré comme acquis* and it will do just fine:

> *Nous pouvons considérer comme acquis ce premier point.*

>> We can take agreement on the first point for granted.

>> We can consider the first point as already established.

par erreur

The term *par erreur* is fairly self evident but it's useful, frequently used, and important to know. It means, naturally enough: by error, in error, by mistake.

> *Pardon, j'ai ouvert cette porte par erreur.*

>> Pardon me, I opened this door in error.

> *Je crois qu'elle l'a fait par erreur.*

>> I believe she did it by mistake.

par mégarde

The term *par mégarde* is similar to *par erreur* but has a different shade of meaning. It means accidently, inadvertently, not on purpose.

The trick I've used to remember it is to think of *regarder* "to look at" and then think of *par mégarde* as "by not looking at" or "by inattention".

A friend subsequently pointed out that *par mégarde* actually comes from *mal garder* or the action of *ne pas prendre garde* (to not be on ones guard). Either way, *par mégarde* means "by inattention".

Elle a renversé la petite table par mégarde.

> She knocked over the little table accidently.

> She knocked over the little table by not paying attention.

Je l'ai laissé à la maison par mégarde.

> I left it at the house accidently.

As you can see, the two terms, *par erreur* and *par mégarde*, can overlap but do have somewhat different meanings. If you said *Elle a renversé la table par erreur* it could imply that she meant to knock over something else instead, or a different table. If you say that she did it *par mégarde* it's clear that it was by accident and inattention.

doucement
en douce

The adverb *doucement* means: softly, slowly, gently, carefully. Consider these examples:

Parlez plus doucement, s'il vous plaît.

> Please speak more slowly (or softly, depending on context).

Nous avons marché doucement pour ne pas faire de bruit.

We walked softly so as not to make any noise.

Il a frappé doucement à la porte.

He knocked softly / gently at the door.

Elle ouvre la porte et elle entre doucement.

She opens the door and enters quietly.

Doucement, les enfants !!!!

Quiet down, kids!

La route descend doucement.

The route descends gradually.

You will use *doucement* often, especially in asking people to talk more slowly. *Lentement* would serve the same purpose, but French people use *doucement*.

On the other hand, the term *en douce* also means "quietly" but has the connotation of "discretely", and even "furtively", "secretly" or "on the sly".

Elle est partie en douce quand il est arrivé.

She slipped away quietly when he arrived.

Elle a continué à lui donner de l'argent en douce.

She continued to give him money on the sly / discretely.

Il se mit à rire en douce.

He started to laugh furtively.

Il a fait un coup en douce.

He played a sneaky trick.

il vaut mieux

Word-for-word meaning "it's worth better to" *il vaut mieux* is translated in practice as "it's better to." You can put any verb after it that you like.

Il vaut mieux is another expression which can be used in a large variety of different circumstances.

Il vaut mieux refuser.

It's better to refuse.

Il vaut mieux arriver tôt.

It's better to arrive early.

The above sentences are built with the infinitive of the next verb *(refuser, arriver)*. However, if you structure the sentence *il vaut mieux que...* you use the subjunctive of the following verb.

il vaut mieux que tu refuses / que vous refusiez.

It's better that you refuse.

Il vaut mieux que nous arrivions tôt.

It's better that we arrive early.

You can also say "It <u>would</u> be better", by using the conditional, saying: *il <u>vaudrait</u> mieux.* For example:

Il vaudrait mieux rester.

It would be better to stay.

Il vaudrait mieux que nous ne venions pas.

It would be better if we didn't come / We had better not come.

manquer

Manquer (to miss) is a difficult verb for English speakers to get a feel for. This is due primarily to the odd structure (odd to us, that is), of the sentences in which you find *manquer* used.

If the sentence starts *il manque* followed by a noun it translates one way:

Il manque deux tasses.

Two cups are missing.

Il manque un bouton à ta chemise.

A button is missing off your shirt

Il manque Marie.

Marie is missing. Marie isn't here.

If you start with the noun it translates differently.

Marie me manque beaucoup.

I miss Marie a lot.

Notice the difference between *Il manque Marie* and *Marie me manque.* The first means "Marie is missing", the second means "I miss Marie". They are totally different.

You have to think of *Marie me manque* as "Marie is missing to me", and then translate it to yourself into vernacular English. Since this is how you say that you miss someone in French, you have to learn it. Here are some more examples to help out:

Marie nous manque.

We miss Marie.

Ma maison / mon chien me manque.

I miss my house/my dog.

Ses chats lui manquent.

He misses his cats.

Finally, note that *manquer* (to miss) can be used in the same sense as the English word "miss" when you talk about missing a train or a flight.

J'ai manqué le train.

I missed the train. (*J'ai manqué le départ du train* is understood. A French synonym would be *J'ai raté le train*).

It's interesting that in English, "to miss" can have three different meanings: He is missing (not here), I miss him (remember him fondly), I missed my flight (didn't arrive on time), and that *manquer* in French can have all three of the same meanings.

Il y a quelque chose qui cloche (là-dedans)

The rather picturesque expression *Il y a quelque chose qui cloche* means that while at first glance an idea, a plan, a proposal, a deal, etc, **appears** okay, you feel, intuit or **suspect** that there is something wrong. You may not be quite able to put your finger on it, but you sense it.

Il y a quelque chose qui cloche can be translated by a variety of vernacular English expressions. For example:

> *Il y a quelque chose qui cloche dans cette affaire.*

> > There is something that's not quite right with this business.

> > There is something wrong with this.

> > There's something about this that doesn't add up.

> *C'est une idée / un plan / une proposition intéressante mais il y a quelque chose qui cloche.*

It's an interesting idea / plan / proposition but there is something wrong / something which doesn't sit right / something which doesn't quite add up / something which doesn't fit.

il y a quelque chose de louche (là-dedans)

While *il ya quelque chose qui cloche là-dedans* means that there's something that's not quite right in that (plan, idea, proposal, etc), *il y a quelque chose de louche là-dedans* means that there is something crooked, fishy, shady, suspicious or dubious about the subject at hand.

> *Il y a quelque chose de louche dans son passé.*

>> There is something suspicious / crooked in his past.

> *Il y a quelque chose de louche dans ces affaires.*

>> There is something shady about those matters.

> *Il y a quelque chose de louche dans cet homme.*

>> There's something suspicious about that man.

Note that each of these sentences could be worded more briefly, with the same ultimate meaning. For example:

> *Il a un passé louche.*

> *Ce sont des affaires louches.*

C'est un homme louche.

pour ainsi dire

The expression *pour ainsi dire* translated word-for-word would be "for thus to speak". In practice it is translated "so to speak". You can use it whenever you would say "so to speak" in English.

> *J'admets que j'ai parlé un peu hâtivement, mais c'est ma nature, pour ainsi dire.*
>
> > I admit that I spoke a bit hastily, but it's my nature, so to speak.

> *Elle pouvait happer au passage, pour ainsi dire, les regards d'autrui.*
>
> > She could snatch on the fly, so to speak, the regards of others. (This example and the previous one are paraphrased from Les Thibault by Roger Martin du Gard. The latter especially is rather poetic and literary.)

> *Il a volé mon idée, pour ainsi dire.*
>
> > He stole my idea, so to speak.

> *Jean a disparu dans la nature, pour ainsi dire.*
>
> > Jean dropped out of sight, so to speak.

à peine
ne...guère

The two expressions *à peine and ne...guère* are closely related and are almost synonyms. *À peine* means hardly, scarcely, barely, *presque pas, très peu,* while *ne...guère* means hardly any, not much, not many, not very, *pas beaucoup, pas très.*

I included the French synonyms above as they seemed to differentiate between the meanings better than the English translations, but it may still sound as if *à peine* and *ne...guère* mean about the same thing. Well actually they do mean about the same thing, but their usage can be different in a few cases. Here are some examples to help illustrate. We'll start with *à peine* :

C'était à peine visible.

It was scarcely visible.

Il arrive à peine.

He's hardly / barely / just arrived

Il peut à peine marcher.

He can barely walk.

J'ai à peine vingt euros.

I have barely twenty euros.

Jean était à peine sorti quand elle est arrivée.

Jean had barely left when she arrived.

Now here are some examples of *ne...guère* :

Je n'aime guère ce restaurant.

I don't like this restaurant much.

On ne voir plus guère ce modèle.

One hardly sees that model anymore.

Ce n'est guère difficile.

It's not very difficult.

Il n'a guère mangé.

He hardly ate.

Nous ne sommes guère invités chez eux.

We are hardly ever invited to their house.

Je n'y ai guère prêté attention.

I scarcely paid any attention to it.

In most cases *à peine* and *ne...guère* could be used interchangeably, for example *Vous n'avez guère mangé /Vous avez à peine mangé.*

However, in a few cases it would be awkward to use the other expression or they would have different meanings. For example, *Il arrive à peine* means "He's just arrived", but *Il n'arrive guère à parler* would mean "He can hardly talk".

sauf ça
hormis ça
à part ça
à l'exception de ça

The word "except" is certainly a key word in everyday conversation. Here are a number of ways to say it in French:

J'ai un peu mal au dos. À part ça, tout va bien.

I have a little back ache. except for that, everything is fine.

Hormis le froid, c'est une belle journée.

Except for the cold, it's a beautiful day.

Je les prendrai tous, à l'exception de celui-là.

I'll take them all, except that one.

Elle n'a rien à elle, sauf ses économies.

She has nothing belonging to her except / besides her savings.

Le magasin est ouvert tous les jours, sauf le dimanche.

The store is open every day except Sundays.

malgré
en dépit de

Malgré and *en dépit de* are two ways to say another common expression, "in spite of".

As with most of the terms I've given you, I've chosen "except" (above) and "in spite of" because you can employ them in a wide variety of settings and circumstances.

Of the two expressions, *malgré* is probably used more commonly than *en dépit de*. Both of them can be translated as "in spite of" or "despite" or "notwithstanding" (*nonobstant*).

Malgré la difficulté il a continué.

Il a continué en dépit de la difficulté.

In spite of / notwithstanding the difficulty he continued.

Il a fait ça en dépit de bon sens.

He did that contrary to commnon sense.

He did that even though it didn't make good sense.

Elle a fait ça malgré sa mère.

Elle a fait ça malgré la réticence de sa mère / les conseils de sa mère.

Elle a fait ça en dépit de la réticence de sa mère / des conseils de sa mère.

She did that in spite of her mother's opposition / advice. (Note that *en dépit* requires a _de_ while *malgré* does not)

Malgré la neige on peut encore conduire.

En dépit de la neige on peut encore conduire.

Despite the snow we can still go by car.

J'ai fait ça malgré moi.

I did that against my will / inspite of myself.

à moins que
à moins de

The expresssions *à moins que* and *à moins de* mean "unless". *À moins que* is followed by the <u>subjunctive</u> of the following <u>verb</u>.

À moins de, on the other hand, is followed by a <u>noun</u> or an <u>expression</u> rather than a verb.

À moins que is used more frequently and we'll look at *à moins que* first:

À moins que je me trompe, il est arrivé à dix-sept heures.

Unless I am mistaken, he arrived at five in the afternoon.

Je préfère ne pas le faire, à moins que vous insistiez.

> I prefer not to do it, unless you insist.

Il va échouer à moins qu'il fasse beaucoup plus d'effort.

> He's going to fail unless he makes a lot more effort.

The above is how one usually talks. However, in written and standard French, with *à moins que* you add a _ne_ before the verb. On the other hand, there is no *pas*. For example:

À moins que je _ne_ me trompe...

...à moins que vous _n'_insistiez.

...à moins qu'il _ne_ fasse...

Let's go on now to *à moins de.*

Nous arriverons à dix-huit heures à moins d'un imprévu.

> We will arrive at six in the afternoon unless something unforeseen happens / barring something unforeseen.

Il va échouer à moins d'un miracle.

> He's going to fail, barring a miracle / unless there's a miracle.

As with most of the terms I've given you, I've chosen these last three expressions (unless, in spite of, except), because they are extremely useful and, above all, versatile.

You can use them in many different circumstances. They are the kind of expressions that you will hear and use every day, rather than once a year.

à la fois

The expression *à la fois* means "at the same time", (or it can sometimes be translated as "both") and is used just like the English expression. For example:

Elle peut être, à la fois, gentille et méchante.

> She can be both charming and wicked / She can be charming and wicked at the same time.

C'est, à la fois, beau et bon marché.

> It's both beautiful and inexpensive / It's beautiful and inexpensive at the same time.

Le verbe anglais, **to patronize,** *peut signifier traiter quelqu'un avec bienveillance apparente mais, à la fois, avec condescendance.*

> The English verb "to patronize" can mean to treat someone with apparent kindness but, at the same time, with condescension.

avoir lieu

Avoir lieu means to take place. It's pretty straightforward:

> *Le concert va avoir lieu demain.*

> The concert will take place tomorrow.

> *L'exposition a lieu cet après-midi.*

> The exhibition is taking place this afternoon.

> *La réunion a eu lieu hier.*

> The meeting took place yesterday.

J'ai bien mangé

In English we would put an adverb like "well" after the main verb and say "I have eaten <u>well</u>". In French the adverb comes after the auxillary verb and before the main verb, as in *j'ai <u>bien</u> mangé.*

If you use the English construction it sounds as awkward to a French ear as if you were to hear a foreigner saying "I have well eaten" in English. You'd understand what they were saying, but you'd think that they don't speak very good English.

In the same way, if you say *"j'ai mangé bien"*, the French people will understand you, but it will sound wrong. My goal is to help you so that your French will sound right.

To reiterate, in French the adverb (such as *bien* or *beau-*

coup) usually comes after the auxillary verb and before the main verb, as in:

On a <u>bien</u> mangé

> We've eaten well. (You do NOT say *"On a mangé bien"*).

Nous avons <u>beaucoup</u> mangé.

> We've eaten a lot.

Ils n'ont <u>rien</u> bu ce soir.

> They drank nothing this evening.

J'ai <u>trop</u> bu.

> I drank too much.

J'ai <u>mal</u> dormi.

> I slept poorly.

Il est <u>subitement</u> parti.

> He left suddenly.

J'ai <u>vraiment</u> vu trois bateaux.

> I really saw three boats.

J'ai <u>jamais</u> mangé autant de raisins / Je n'ai <u>jamais</u> mangé autant de raisins.

> I have never eaten so many grapes. (NOT: *Je n'ai mangé jamais tant de raisins*).

This holds as well when you use other auxillary verbs like *pouvoir, vouloir* and *aller*. The adverb still comes after the auxillary verb and before the main verb:

> *Nous allons <u>bien</u> manger chez Jean.*
>
>> We will eat well at Jean's house. (Or it can mean "We are <u>really</u> going to eat at Jean's house", as you will remember from the discussion of *bien* as a word used to intensify.)

> *On peut <u>bien</u> entendre.*
>
>> One can hear well.

> *Ils vont <u>bientôt</u> arriver.*
>
>> They will arrive soon.

> *Cela veut <u>aussi</u> dire...*
>
>> That also means...

However, when there is no auxillary verb, as in the present tense, future tense, or conditional tense, the adverb goes after the verb as in English:

> *Elle mange <u>beaucoup</u>.*

> *Il boit <u>trop</u>.*

> *Elle parle <u>peu</u>.*

> *On mange <u>bien</u> dans ce restaurant.*

> *Nous mangerons <u>bien</u>.*

Elle ne dira <u>rien</u>.

Il parle français et il parle <u>aussi</u> italien

Note, however, that when *beaucoup, trop* and *peu,* don't modify the verb but modifie some object, they usually come after the main verb, instead of between the auxillary and the main verb.

This sounded very complicated when I stated it in words but it is very simple when I illustrate it with a couple of examples:

J'ai <u>trop</u> bu. - **BUT** - *J'ai bu <u>trop de vin</u>.*

Elle a <u>peu</u> mangé. - **BUT** - *Elle a mangé <u>peu de carottes.</u>*

comme tout

This very nice little expression emphasizes an adjective. *Comme tout* is always positive and can be translated as: very, really, extremely, incredibly. (This is casual rather than formal French, of course).

Elle est gentille comme tout !

She's really nice.

C'est joli comme tout.

It's very pretty.

Leur chaton est mignon comme tout.

Their kitten is as cute as anything.

C'était facile comme tout.

It was incredibly easy!

Note: Don't confuse this expression with *tout comme* which we addressed earlier in the book and which means "just like".

comme ci, comme ça

While we are on *comme*, the little expression *comme ci, comme ça* means "so-so", "neither good nor bad". It's easy to remember and easy to use.

Comment vas-tu ? --- Comme ci, comme ça.

How are you? --- So-so.

comme (meaning "in the way of")

The word *comme* can also mean "in the way of". What I mean by "in the way of" is also difficult to explain in words, but it is easily illustrated with a couple of examples:

Qu'est-ce que vous avez de nouveau aujourd'hui comme fruit ?

What do you have new today in the way of fruit.

Que veux-tu comme boisson / dessert ?

What would you like in the way of a drink/ dessert.

Comme bagage, il n'avait qu'un sac à dos.

In the way of baggage, he had only a back-pack.

n'avoir rien à voir avec

The useful expression *n'avoir rien à voir avec* means "to have nothing to do with" (someone or something). It says that the two things referred to have nothing to do with each other. For example:

Le mot français, une caution, n'a rien à voir avec le mot anglais, caution.

The French noun, *une caution*, has nothing to do with the English word caution.

Cela n'a rien à voir avec lui.

That has nothing to do with him.

Ça n'a rien à voir avec cette proposition.

That has nothing to do with this proposal.

Note that this term is different from *n'y être pour rien (je n'y suis pour rien)*, which we dealt with earlier in the book.

While *n'y être pour rien* can also be translated "to have nothing to do with it", *n'y être pour rien* is a denial of responsibility as in:

Je n'y suis pour rien / Elle n'y est pour rien.

I had nothing to do with it / She had nothing to do with it.

while *n'avoir rien à voir avec* means simply that the two things are not related:

> *Ça n'a rien à voir avec cette proposition.*

Pas de problème !
Pas de souci !

The expression *Pas de problème* means "No problem!", just as you might expect. You use it as you would use "No problem!" in English. For example:

> *Je crains que nous ne soyons quinze minutes en retard. --- Pas de problème, nous vous attendrons.*
>
> I'm afraid that we'll be about fifteen minutes late. --- No problem! We'll be expecting you.

> *Je n'ai pas de monnaie. --- Pas de problème. Tu paieras demain.*
>
> I don't have the change. - No problem. You can pay tomorrow.

Pas de problème is, of course, an abbreviation for *Il n'y a pas de problème*, and is thus casual language.

Another common expression is *Pas de souci !* which has a similar, but not exactly identical, meaning. We discussed *Pas de souci !* earlier as an abbreviation of *Ne te fait pas de souci.*

Specifically, you could translate *Pas de souci !* as "No worry!" or "Don't worry yourself about it!". Most of the time you could use *Pas de problème* or *Pas de souci* interchangeably. For example, in the illustration just above, you could say:

> ...*Pas de souci. Tu paieras demain.*

In both languages, *Pas de problème !* and "No problem!" can also simply mean *D'accord !* or "Okay!". Note the the three examples just below. In each of these *Pas de problème !* would be translated by "No problem" or "Okay".

> *Puis-je entrer maintenant ? --- Pas de problème.*

> *Est-ce que tu peux venir demain ? --- Pas de problème.*

> *Puis-je manger une pomme ? --- Pas de problème.*

There is a nuance of difference between *Pas de problème* and *Pas de souci. Pas de souci* which means "don't worry" just wouldn't be as appropriate a respnse when someone is asking if they can eat an apple.

On the other hand, note the example below, in which *Pas de souci* is used to tell someone specifically not to worry about a set of circumstances.

> *Nous voudrions bien vous inviter à rester manger avec nous, mais nous avions prévu de manger les restes et je crains qu'il n'y ait pas assez.*

--- Pas de souci. On se contentera de ce qu'il y a.

> We would like very much to invite you to stay and eat with us, but we had planned to eat left-overs and I'm afraid that there won't be enough. --- Don't worry yourself about it. We'll be content with whatever there is.

You could respond:

--- Pas de problème. On se contentera de ce qu'il y a.

> No problem. We'll be content with whatever there is.

and no one would think twice about your choice of expressions, but *Pas de souci !* is a better choice here, as you are really telling someone not to worry.

d'ailleurs

D'ailleurs means "besides" or "besides which".

Since *ailleurs*, by itself, means "elsewhere" in a physical sense, it's difficut to see how the meaning of *d'ailleurs* came from that of *ailleurs*. It undoubtably did at one time, but the meanings have grown apart.

The word "besides" has two different senses in English. The **first meaning** of besides in English is "in addition". This sense of besides is usually translated by *en outre* or *de plus*:

Je voudrais quelques pommes, et en outre/et de plus, je voudrais quelques poires.

Besides the apples I'd like some pears.

I'd like some apples, besides which I'd like some pears.

The **second meaning** of besides in English, is "moreover", as if the speaker has had an additional thought addressing another aspect of the subject. It is this sense of besides which is usually translated as *d'ailleurs*. For example:

C'était une vraie bêtise! D'ailleurs, si tu étais resté chez nous comme je t'ai dit, ceci ne serait jamais arrivé.

It was a stupid thing to do. And besides, if you had stayed home as had told you, this wouldn't have ever happened.

Je ne l'ai pas vue, et d'ailleurs, c'était de sa faute.

I didn't see her. And besides, it was her fault. (After an accident).

piger

Piger is a very slangy verb which is the equivalent of "to get it" or "to understand it" in English. You wouldn't use it in any kind of formal situation, but it is commonly used in speech among young people.

Tu piges ? or *Est-ce que tu piges ?*

Do you get it?

J'ai beau expliquer, il ne pige rien.

Even though I explained, he didn't get any of it.

J'ai pas pigé ce qu'il a dit.

I didn't get what he said.

The *ne* was dropped here from *je n'ai pas pigé*. Since *piger* is slangy in itself, if you are using it in conversation the context would probably be very informal.

de fil en aiguille

From a very slangy expression we move to a more classical one. *De fil en aiguille* literally means "from thread to needle" and implies that one thing happened after another by a natural progression. It can be translated as "one thing leading to another" or "little by little" or "gradually".

J'ai vu les cerisiers en fleur, et de fil en aiguille, j'ai songé à Claire.

I saw the cherry trees in flower and, one thing leading to another, I thought of Claire

...and, little by little, I thought of Claire

Peu à peu, de fil en aiguille, il m'en a dit d'avantage.

Little by little, he gradually told me more.

De fil en aiguille, nous avons commencé à parler de Paris.

One thing leading to another, we started to talk about Paris.

Little by little, we started to talk about Paris.

au fil du temps

This expression uses a different meaning of the word *le fil*. In this case it means "the flow", instead of "the thread". Thus *au fil du temps* means "as time flows by" or "with the flow of time" or "over the course of time". It doesn't really mean the same thing at all as *de fil en aiguille*. Variations are *au fil des heures, au fil des jours* (as the hours go by, as the days go by).

Au fil des jours il a beaucoup amelioré sa déxtérité.

Over the course of days he greatly improved his skill / dexterity.

As the days went by, he greatly improved his skill / dexterity.

La santé de Pierre s'améliore au fil des jours.

Pierres's health improved as the days went by.

138

There are other expressions using *le fil* in the sense of "the flow". For example:

> *le fil des événements*
>
>> the course of events
>
> *suivre (ou) perdre le fil de la conversation*
>
>> to follow (or) to lose the <u>flow</u> of the conversation

It's interesting that in English you can use "thread" figuratively and translate this expression as:

>> to follow (or) to lose the <u>thread</u> of the conversation

entre-temps

Entre-temps means "meanwhile" or "in the meantime". You can use it whenever you use "meanwhile" or "in the meantime".

> *Entre-temps j'avais réussi à finir le travail.*
>
>> In the meanwhile I had finished the work / job.
>
> *Entre-temps il m'est arrivé de rencontrer M. Boucher au Café de la Poste.*
>
>> In the meanwhile I happened to meet Mr. Boucher at the Café de la Poste.

tenir le coup

Literally *tenir le coup* literally means "to hold up under the blow". It can be translated as to hold up under, or to withstand the stress or the blow. It's proper French and you can use it anywhere.

> *Je lui ai annoncé que son frère était mort et il a bien réussi à tenir le coup.*
>
> > I explained to him that his brother is dead and he held up well.

> *J'ai travaillais dans un grand magasin mais je ne tenais pas le coup.*
>
> > I worked in a big department store but I couldn't take the stress / but I couldn't hold up.

à souhait

The expression *à souhait* (pronounced "ah soo-ay") acts as an adverb and means "as much as one could want" or "as well as one could want".

> *On a mangé à souhait.*
>
> > We ate as much as we wanted / as much as we could eat.

> *Tout s'est passé à souhait.*
>
> > Everything went as well as we could desire.

bref

We can handle *bref* very quickly as it is actually intuitive in English. *Bref* means "briefly", "in short" or "in brief" or "to sum up in a few words". All of these are just as you might expect. *Bref* is a synonym of *enfin*, is proper French, and can be used anywhere.

Bref, ça ne sert à rien.

In short, that serves no purpose.

avoir la flemme de faire quelque chose

Avoir la flemme de faire quelque chose means "to be too lazy to do it" or "to not want to bother to do it" or "to feel it's too much trouble to do it".

Si vous passez à la boulangerie, est-ce que vous pouvez achetez du pain pour moi ? J'ai la flemme d'aller en ville aujourd'hui.

If you pass a bakery, could you buy a bread for me, I don't have the energy to go into town today.

Nous avons beaucoup travaillé ces derniers jours. J'ai la flemme de tailler les oliviers aujourd'hui.

We've worked a lot the past few days. I'm not up to trimming the olive trees today.

jadis
naguère
d'antan
autrefois

Jadis (the "s" is pronounced) and *naguère* are a couple of words that are a bit literary, but are very nice to use. They give you ways to speak about the past. *Jadis* means in times past, formerly, or once, while *naguère* means not long ago. *Jadis* is used for the distant past, while *naguère* is used for the recent past.

> *Jadis ces cabanons en pierre abritaient les bergers par mauvais temps.*

> > In olden times these stone cabins sheltered shepherds in bad weather.

> > Once these stone cabins sheltered shepherds in bad weather.

> *Pour la fête les femmes portent les costumes de jadis.*

> > For the festival the women wear costumes of olden days.

> *Naguère c'était un joli champs ici, et regarde maintenant, quel lotissement laid.*

> > Not long ago it was a pretty field here, and look now, an ugly development.

> *Mes compagnons de naguère sont tous partis ailleurs.*

My recent companions have all left for other places.

I'll throw in one more similar word, even more poetical than *jadis* and *naguère*. This is *d'antan* which means of olden days.

Mais où sont les neiges d'antan ?

But where are the snows of olden days / of yesteryear? (François Villon)

Finally *autrefois* is the current, ordinary, plain, bread-and-butter word which means formerly, in the past, or once.

Autrefois ces cabanons en pierre abritaient les bergers par mauvais temps.

Mes compagnons d'autrefois sont tous partis ailleurs.

I'm afraid that find *autrefois* a colorless word without the charm of the first three, which I prefer to use when appropriate, but perhaps that's just a matter of personal taste.

facultatif

There is a French word *optionnel* meaning optional, but it is not often used. The word that you are likely to hear all the time is *facultatif*. Since *facultatif* is frequently used, and not at all an intuitive word for an anglophone, I thought I should include it.

Les classes de l'après-midi sont facultatives.

The afternoon classes are optional.

Un pourboire est facultatif ici.

A tip is optional here.

traiter en
traiter de

Traiter en and *traiter de* are expressions that you will hear frequently. *Traiter quelqu'un en* means "to treat someone <u>as</u>" or "to treat someone <u>as if</u>". For example:

Il m'a traité en intrus.

He treated me as (if I was) an intruder.

Elle l'a traité en fils.

She treated him as if he were her son.

On the other hand *traiter quelqu'un <u>de</u>* means to call someone a name.

Elle m'a traité d'idiot devant mes amis.

She called me an idiot in front of my friends,

Il l'a traitée de tous les noms.

He called her every name in the book.

Note that *elle l'a traité <u>en</u> idiot* means she **treated him as** an idiot, while *elle l'a traité <u>d</u>'idiot* means she **called him** an idiot.

Note also that *traiter* can also be used without the *en* or the *de* :

> *Il m'a très mal traité.*

>> He treated me very badly.

> *Elle a très mal traité sa fille.*

>> She treated her daughter very badly.

> *Il l'a traitée comme une chienne.*

>> He treated her like a dog.

tiré par les cheveux

Tiré par les cheveux means "far-fetched" or "unlikely". It's a rather picturesque expression, literally translating as "pulled by the hairs".

> *Cette théorie est un peu tirée pas les cheveux.*

>> That theory is a bit far-fetched / is a bit of a stretch.

faute de mieux

Just as you would expect, *faute de mieux* means "for lack of better".

> *Il a bu, faute de mieux, un mauvais vin.*

>> He drank a poor wine, for lack of better.

bel et bien

The expression *bel et bien* acts as an adverb and means that something happened, or was true, "after all" when it had been uncertain or in doubt.

> *Il a bel et bien tenu sa promesse.*
>
> He kept his promise after all.
>
> *Ils sont bel et bien arrivés à l'heure.*
>
> They arrived on time after all.
>
> *La magnifique théière était bel et bien en porcelaine.*
>
> The magnificent teapot was indeed in porcelain.

après coup

Après coup, means after the fact, afterwards, looking back, after the event.

> *Après coup, j'ai pensé à toutes les bonnes réponses que j'aurais pu donner à ses remarques.*
>
> Afterwards, I thought of all the good responses that I could have given to his remarks.

cela ne tient pas debout

Cela ne tient pas debout means that it doesn't stand up to examination, it doesn't hold water.

Cette histoire ne tient pas debout.

> That story doesn't hold water. That story doesn't make sense.

en vouloir

The expression *en vouloir à quelqu'un* can be translated as "to hold something against someone" or "to hold a grudge against someone" or "to be angry at someone". It's a common verb form and it's proper French. You can use it anywhere.

> *Il m'en veut à cause de...*

> > He holds a grudge against me because of...

> *Ne m'en veux pas.*

> > Don't be angry at me because of it.

> > Don't hold it against me.

> *Il en veut à sa soeur de ce qu'elle à dit.*

> > He's still angry at his sister because of what she said.

à l'improviste

The expression *à l'improviste* is related to the verb improvise and means: on the spur of the moment, without advance planning.

Est-ce que vous pouvez rester manger avec nous.
Ce sera un repas à l'improviste.

> Can you stay and eat with us. It will be an improvised meal.

> Can you stay and eat with us. It will be a spur of the moment meal.

Nous avons décidé d'y aller, à l'improviste.

Nous avons, à l'improviste, décidé d'y aller.

> We decided on the spur of the moment to go there.

Jean est passé chez nous à l'improviste.

> Jean came by our house without warning / on the spur of the moment.

un drôle de

The expression *un drôle de* is frequently heard. It's used to designate a funny, strange, odd or peculiar thing or person and is often said with humor.

C'est un drôle de chat.

> That's a funny cat / That's an odd cat.

Quel drôle de type.

> What an odd character.

Quelle drôle d'idée.

What a strange idea.

pas mal

The expression *pas mal* has two different uses. First it can refer to an amount and mean "quite a bit".

> *Tailler tous les arbres m'a pris pas mal de temps.*
>
>> To trim all the trees took me quite a bit of time.

> *Elle a pas mal de bijoux.*
>
>> She has quite a lot of jewelry.

The second meaning for *pas mal* is as an appreciation, similar to the English "That's not bad!"

> *Qu'est-ce que tu penses de cette robe ? --- Pas mal !*
>
>> What do you think of this dress? --- Not bad!

> *C'est pas mal de tout.*
>
>> That's not bad at all.

laisse tomber !

The expression *laisser tomber* translates literally as "to let fall" or "to allow to fall". In practice, referring to **an object**, *laisser tomber* means "to drop":

Quand il l'a vue entrer la pièce, surpris, il a laissé tomber son livre.

When he saw her enter the room he dropped his book in surprise.

When he saw her enter the room he let the book fall in surprise.

The usage that I want to describe to you though is the figurative. When someone says *laisse tomber !* referring to **a subject** of conversation he is saying "Drop it !" just as one would say in English. It means that he or she doesn't want to discuss it any longer. Similarly if the person is referring to **an activity** it also means "Drop it, let it go for now".

Maman, si je suis très sage aujourd'hui, puis-je aller au cinéma demain ? --- J'ai déjà dit "Non!" trois fois. Laisse tomber !

Mommy, if I am very good today, can I go to the movies tomorrow? --- I've already said "No!" three times. Drop the subject!

Je vais finir de tailler cet olivier. --- Oh, laisse tomber. On le fera demain.

I'm going to finish trimming this olive tree. --- Oh, let it go for now, we'll do it tomorrow.

We'll drop the subject of idioms and expressions on this note and bring this edition of the book to a close. I hope that you have found it interesting and useful.

List of References

I used the following reference books to supplement my knowledge from everyday reading and conversation in the preparation of this book.

Harper Collins French Concise Dictionary, Second Edition, Harper Collins, 2000

Harrap's Shorter Dictionnaire, Anglais-Français Français-Anglais, 7th Edition, Chambers Harrap, 2004

Webster's New World Dictionary, Second College Edition, Simon and Schuster, 1982

Le Petit Robert, Dictionnaire Alphabétique et Analogique de la Langue Française, Dictionnaires Le Robert, 1993

Le Petit Larousse, Grand Format, Larousse, 2001

Dictionary 1.0.1, Apple Computer 2005

Alphabetical Listing